GRAMMAR
FOR
GROWNUPS

GRAMMAR
FOR
GROWNUPS

Val Dumond

HarperPerennial
A Division of HarperCollinsPublishers

The Library of Congress has catalogued the hardcover edition of this book as follows:
Dumond, Val.
    Grammar for grownups/Val dumond.—1st ed.
      p. cm.
    Includes index.
    ISBN 0-06-270054-5
    1. English language—Grammar—1950– . I. Title.
PE1112.D85 1993
428.2—dc20   92-33204

ISBN 0-06-272043-0 (pbk)
94 95 96 97 98 PS/RRD 10 9 8 7 6 5 4

Contents

Introduction

Wouldn't our communication lives be simplified if only there were a single authority, a Chief of Grammar, a National Grammar Archive, a single set of rules to dictate how our language is spoken and written? If there were such a ruling body, we surely would have unearthed it by now.

There isn't.

There are no 21 Rules of Grammar as there are the Ten Commandments, the Bill of Rights, the Magna Carta, and the Constitution.

Do you want to know why? Because nobody knows all the rules. Yes! It's true. Nowhere is there a set of grammar rules that everyone can turn to because everyone cannot agree on what the rules are.

Yes, experts and specialists abound. Many have tried to put down all the rules in one place, end to end, but managed only to dredge up controversy among the other experts. Difficult as it may be to believe, grammar specialists differ—a lot! (They differ on whether or not *a lot* is a usable phrase.)

The reason for this discord in the ranks of grammarians is that the American English language comes to us through evolution (God, yes!), not creation. The language has evolved from the generation before us, and the generation before them, and for generations back to the roots of civilization and the first spoken word (which must have been *don't*). It is still evolving.

The American language comes to us from every other language in the world and is inserted, squeezed, pushed, dropped, finagled or pounded into common usage. *Common usage* means *the way people use it every day*. Unlike Latin or Greek, our language comes to us à la carte, not as a structured, organized convention.

Therefore, how could there possibly be one set of rules?

There can't. Of course, some basics are generally recognized. These help make the language inter-usable as a means of communication. However, there are many gray areas.

Because:
* few specialists agree among themselves,
* language constantly changes,
* different groups use their own adaptations of the language,
* communication needs (goals, objectives, strategies) vary accordingly.

For instance:

Mark Twain's language was that of a story teller, using dialects and regional words, and syntax. The great writers—Shakespeare, the Brontes, Hemingway, Faulkner, Austen, Steinbeck, Uris, Mailer, Oates—tell their stories using their own words, punctuation, and beliefs about grammar.

Advertising agencies and public relations representatives have their own set of techniques to persuade and sell ideas to motivate others.

Computer people have developed their own language to transmit a new technology in a new environment.

Sports writers use a slang terminology indecipherable to the uninitiated. A sports bar during Monday night football sounds as alien to the non-sports fan as the world of academia does to the untutored.

Military jargon, clipped, direct, symbolizing instant recognition and response, has its own language rules.

The poet's language is full of metaphoric music with meanings unique to the poet and the philosopher, a language where the meaning of life supersedes the meaning of living.

An attorney's language is aimed at dotting *i*'s and crossing *t*'s to a degree that takes it beyond common comprehension. *Medical* language, likewise, is incomprehensible to the lay person. Attorneys take seven years to learn to disguise their communication; doctors take ten or more to obscure theirs.

Workers in their own areas of operation—auto assembly lines, design drawing boards, bars, antique shops, mines, fishing craft, grain fields, stables, artist garrets, symphony halls, churches, insurance offices, stock markets, meat markets, schools—all speak their own languages and follow their own rules of grammar.

Who can say what is right or wrong, what is correct or incorrect?

The language of the professional grammarian—found in departments of English and other languages at universities and colleges—offers all kinds of answers about what is right and wrong. It is as difficult to find agreement among them as it is to find agreement among sports fans as to the most valuable player, the leading team, or the best game.

Students sometimes accuse me of reacting to a heated grammar debate like the character Diane on the TV show "Cheers," because I get as excited about grammar as she does about English Lit. Grammar is not a dead set of rules to be endured. Grammar is alive, changing, controversial. Grammar requires attention and energy to catch hold of it. In return for using it well, writers find they are better understood in less time with less need for clarification.

In preparing this book, my sources have been the communicators I find around me—on television and radio, in newspapers, among speakers, debaters, friends, colleagues, strangers, and grammar *experts*—all of whom provided the examples of grownup language used here. Most of them were overheard speaking for themselves.

In my first class of college freshman English (re-named Communications), a tuned-in professor assigned us to listen to the ways people talk informally—at home, in stores, in restaurants, over meals or coffee, at rest, at play, in class, or even sitting on the lawn—wherever people used words to communicate. We were to bring examples of *speech* back to class. I've been carrying out that assignment ever since. This book gives you a fairly accurate recap of what I learned.

The first thing I learned is that people don't talk grammar. They don't talk language. They don't even talk words. They talk ideas.

Another thing I learned is that what was taught back in grade school had little to do with the way our language is used, although it was a good start for a complex subject.

Many years later while teaching basic grammar to GED students, I learned the most important lesson. In reviewing all those grade school rules, I found I had been using most of that stuff for years without knowing why. By refreshing the basics in preparation for teaching that class, I refreshed my own sense of language, with the results that my command of words has improved. Now, when I hesitate—*Do I use a comma here? Do I use a plural or singular? Which verb tense is appropriate? How is this word spelled?*—now I have the guidelines I need.

I also have the freedom to improvise, create, and add my own relaxed style to the way I use language. This book offers a combination of guidelines and creative language use for you to start building your own style of speaking and writing.

I must thank Miss Miller, my third grade teacher, and all the Miss Millers in all the elementary grades for providing the basics which we use until we grow up. I thank my professor, Marian Hawkins, and all the open-minded college communication specialists who recognize the need to adapt the rules to usage guidelines. I also thank all the language users whose words are repeated in this book, people overheard talking their own ideas.

                                                        Val Dumond

Part 1

RECALLING THE PARTS OF SPEECH

Grammar is not for kids. You were taught the rules of grammar in a way similar to the way you were taught sex, before you had a chance to experiment. Rules, therefore, became meaningless until you had some experience for reference.

Adults can look at grammar (and sex) in a new light. You may have the knack of it now because you've had a chance to try it out, but you may need a good review of the guidelines to be sure you're using them to the best advantage. Now suddenly, as grownups, all that stuff you learned in grade school begins to make sense.

Most writers have little trouble using the language. Like most grownups, they don't think much about grammar until an opportunity comes up to review the basics. Then comes the eye-opener. "Aha! That's why I do that!" you hear them say. Now whenever they write themselves into a corner, they have the grammatical guidelines to get out.

How did you learn to talk? By listening and copying. How did you learn to write? By following a teacher's admonitions about "gramm-err!" Back in Miss Miller's third grade class, I don't know who wasn't devastated by the papers returned with red pock marks all over them. The essays kids so proudly put together from their own thoughts were handed back with gaudy red notes telling them to "do it over, spell the words right, use punctuation!" With this kind of start in language, it's no wonder that many people grow up apologizing, "I'm a bad speller; I never did know where to put the commas; I always hated writing."

Grammar doesn't have to mean pain anymore. Now that you've grown up you are ready to use this marvelous communications tool, to take a new look at an old subject, pick up a few reminders of what you already know, and—at last!—to write and speak with the satisfaction of handling the language well. Grownups are ready to enjoy grammar.

Do you remember your Miss Miller back in elementary school talking about those horrible predicates and verbals and genders and clauses? At the time you probably were more interested in bicycling and tennis and baseball and building tree houses. You'll be surprised at how much has stayed with you.

Grownups reviewing grammar are astonished at how much they already know but have forgotten. All through this book, you will find yourself easily recalling the guidelines you need to write well, but which made no sense until you review them with an adult mind.

Is good language use important? You bet it is. But it isn't restricted, confined, or simply black and white; it's flexible. Still, grammar provides a structure to communication that, with its nuances and shades of meaning, contributes to the enjoyment of writing, reading, speaking and listening.

Without punctuation and the guidelines of grammar, we'd get lost in the jumble of words. Without the use of reasonable guidelines and consistent standards, communication would be meaningless. The better your ability to use the guidelines, the more fine-tuned and clear will be your message.

Someone once said that without the misuse of grammar and punctuation, lawyers would be out of work. On more than one occasion, millions of dollars, legal decisions and enormous prestige have ridden on the placement of a single comma. People who can handle words skillfully earn professional respect. They gain self-confidence and impress clients; they are the ones moving up to better jobs.

Children need rules in grade school. They provide structure, security, and foundation. Grownups need guidelines. Furthermore, they can be relied on to make choices for themselves. As a grownup, you need to know that you have the right to stretch the old rules, enhance them, even make up your own. As long as the goal is to improve communications, go for it. Just be sure to throw in a modicum of consistency.

Yes, grammar is an art. Yes, grammar is a skill. Yes, grammar (like sex) holds out the challenge to do it well. And yes, grammar is fun!

TWO PARTS—EQUAL BUT SEPARATE

Writing is a two-part process. Unfortunately, most of us didn't learn that in grade school. The first part is composition, organizing information into thoughts and ideas to be communicated. We won't concern ourselves too much with the creative writing process here, other than to look at better ways to project ideas clearly.

The second part is what we're concerned with in this book—the use of the right word forms, spelled adequately, shaped into usable sentences and punctuated, and the use of the best guidelines to aid in understanding. This whole process is what we call grammar, and it comes after the creative writing part. When we try to apply grammar and spelling rules at the same time that we're composing ideas, we risk fracturing the message. How can we possibly explain a complex situation or describe a brilliant idea when we're obsessed with whether or not to use an apostrophe inside or outside the quotation marks?

Corporate personnel who take courses in business writing most often actually want a course in grammar. Business executives and support staff alike are out of touch with the elementary guidelines they learned back in school. Many, confused about commas for instance, will either scatter them indiscriminately throughout their work or refuse to use them at all. Those who are uncertain about spelling whine about their inability to spell and ask someone else to type their work.

Perhaps for the first time, American language users are learning to create their ideas on paper with complete disregard for rules. Then, afterwards, they can edit their work with an eye on grammar guidelines and dictionary spelling. The separation of grammar from creativity is as important an idea as separation of church and state, and has not been emphasized sufficiently in the teaching of grammar.

DICTIONARIES

Believe it or not, dictionaries follow speech, not the other way around. When people began to talk, they didn't have dictionaries or grammar books. They got along as best as they could by making sounds that later would turn up in dictionaries.

Our language still functions this way. We continue to make sounds that aren't in the dictionaries. If more people make the same sounds, the things catch on and soon, lo and behold, they appear in a dictionary.

Not all dictionaries will insert the new word at the same time. Some dictionary writers wait until everybody knows the word and are using it before they consider adding it to their list of words.

Select your dictionary carefully. Try out a couple before you latch onto one particular model. Different word users prefer different styles of dictionary writing, in the same way they prefer their own kind of novel.

Shop for a dictionary the same way you shop for a word processing program.

A hint from successful writers: Don't trust the programs that provide grammar rules and spell checks. Oh, they're great for catching obvious errors, but they are not as fine-tuned as you will be once you review the guidelines for yourself. In addition, a computer doesn't have your style.

Neither does a dictionary. It is only a guide, not the highest authority of grammar or usage. You, the communicator, have the role of deciding what to use and what to discard. Dictionaries use such codes as *archaic, slang, optional* behind words they are unsure of. Take those codes to mean it's up to you!

BOOK FORMAT

This book emphasizes grammar as a separate activity: to improve written communication. The concepts have effectively helped to improve the grammar (and writing) of many business people over the years in many areas of commerce—customer service, marketing, sales, personnel and administration—as well as that of people writing business letters, employee appraisals, and reports.

Grammar For Grownups is divided into three parts:

- Recalling the Parts of Speech
- Punctuation—The Guideposts of the Road
- Creating Your Own Style

A workbook section at the end of each chapter provides space for individual notes and practice in using what has just been reviewed. People learn best when they have a space to make notes about what strikes them as important, different or something-I-don't-want-to-forget. And the exercises show just how easy it is to handle language with confidence.

The first part provides a review of the major parts of speech: naming words (nouns and pronouns), verbs, modifying words (adjectives and adverbs), prepositions, conjunctions, interjections, and verbals. The names of these parts of speech are distinguished from their functions. A noun does other things than act as a subject, for instance.

The second part reviews the punctuation marks that serve as guideposts to writing clear messages. You'll find simple ideas to help you use punctuation as effectively in written correspondence and business reports as you do in memos and refrigerator notes.

The third part deals with putting all the guidelines to work in getting across the right message to the right person. You'll discover the importance of aiming your message at the expected audience for the stated purpose. You'll find hints for improving spelling, using numbers, reducing sexism in language, structuring sentences and building paragraphs, as well as selling ideas. You'll take a healthy look at many of the areas of word usage that communicators trip over.

In each chapter, you'll review the more commonly agreed upon guidelines and look at some of the common pitfalls. Many times, all it takes is a new and grownup look at a guideline to provide an understanding of why you use words the way you do. "Aha, now I know why some words are capitalized, and others aren't."

You may notice that many words can turn up with several names, meaning they can serve in more than one capacity. A word may be a noun and a verb (report), an adjective and an adverb (daily). Words can be stretched and altered to function in several capacities: operate (v.), operator, operation (n.), operational (adj.), operationally (adv.), operative (n. and adj.). A noun may serve in a sentence as either subject or object.

Best of all, the intimidating technical terminology of grammar has been reduced. When it isn't absolutely necessary to use words like transitive, intransitive, participle, retroactive conjunctivitis, preterit, declension, restrictive and nonrestrictive, we won't. If you've ever had to parse a sentence or conjugate a verb, relax. There'll be none of that here. As often as possible, terms are used that easily define the function. You will find the word *rule* used sparingly, if at all.

Simple remembering tools are offered to make dealing with troublesome word usage even easier the next time it comes up. Each chapter closes with a few exercises to challenge you and help reinforce what you've read. Answers to the exercises are found in the Appendix.

You'll benefit from this book if you are in business, a professional writer, a classroom teacher, writing instructor, or someone who just wants to use language in the way that gives them an edge. When you talk well, you are listened to with more credibility and respect.

Business people who have to write reports, letters, memos in the course of a routine business day are always in need of guidelines, ways to write more efficiently (and maybe even have fun while they're doing it).

Professional writers might find they can discard many bad habits carried around since grade school. After re-reading the guidelines, who knows, some of the pros might find a new idea or two to incorporate into their own work.

Classroom teachers may want to review their curricula for writing or language classes. They may find that good writing habits can be developed through subjects other than language or grammar courses. Teachers of science, math, history, and even physical education can offer opportunities to improve their students' communication skills by improving their use of language. Teachers are grownups too, and many of them haven't reviewed grammar since they were in grade school.

And, if you are a *writing instructor*, please use this book to set up classes for other grownups. Don't keep this stuff secret—share the news of good and flexible grammar with as many others as you can.

1

Places to Go, Things to See, People to Meet

NOUNS

Nouns are the words that name people, places, and things. People and places are easy; we can see them. And some of the things that we can see are easy to name. But nouns are also the things we can't see, like freedom, wind, peace, timing, ethics, difficulty, and noise, and they are more difficult to identify and name. This chapter addresses all kinds of nouns and how to handle capitalization (Proper Nouns), plurals, possessives, verbals and noun/verb agreement.

What do you think of when you think of nouns? People, places and things. Miss Miller got that point across so well that it's difficult to repeat those nouns in any other order.

Nouns are the naming words, the words to which we attach labels. Americans take great delight in attaching labels to all kinds of objects whether or not they can be seen. Nouns are the objects or ideas people talk about.

Naming things you can see is easy: tree, dog, car, flower, sky, mother, man, person, building, park, city, star, sun. Naming things you cannot see is fairly common: feelings such as sadness, wonder, anger, joy; or traits such as honor, trust, bravery. To label ideas—indoctrination, discrimination, power, challenge, morale, silence—is more difficult.

Nouns can be generic, as in city or child or park, or specific, as in Chicago, Kim, or Kennywood Park. When they are specific, they are called proper nouns, and are capitalized to show that you're talking about a certain city, child or park.

CAPITALIZING NOUNS

Capitalized words command more attention than other words and can be confusing when they are used only for that purpose. We aren't always sure whether or not to capitalize city police, a child care center, or the park attendant. Perhaps, the following guidelines will help.

Capitalize a noun when referring to a particular person, place or thing when it has its own name. Capitalize the word company, city or park only when referring to a specific company, city or park. If you work for the city of Denver and wish to refer to other city workers, you may capitalize City workers. The same guideline applies for other such words: company, state, county, federal. Do not capitalize such a term that precedes a proper name (city of Denver, state of Colorado). People who work for government agencies or groups often choose to capitalize the word all the time. That's a matter of choice by the agency or group.

One simple guideline suggests capitalizing words like state, federal government, nation, or city when it is preceded by *the* and when it substitutes for the actual name of the state, federal government, nation or city. (Since the State asked for taxes . . .) However, generally use lower case letters when preceded by a possessive: this company, our city, their organization. Whether or not to capitalize federal is a personal choice unless you work for an agency that insists you always put it in caps.

Style Manuals

Many of these minor options are best settled by using a style manual. Ask your employer for guidelines. They're called stylebooks, style manuals, or style sheets and many organizations compile their own. Someone sometime has made the decision to capitalize or not capitalize, so that it's not up to you. Just follow the style guidelines. If your company or agency doesn't have such a book, ask for one to be furnished, either prepared in-house or purchased. Since most newspapers use style books to ensure that all writing for the publication is consistent, many big newspapers have published their own style manuals, available through book stores or libraries.

A style manual will ensure that everyone writing for a single company or publication can look up answers to dilemmas of capitalization, punctuation, use of technical words, abbreviations, and other questions of consistency that may arise. It helps maintain a singular image to the outside world, as if everyone who writes for the company is working together.

People

Ranks and titles are capitalized if they are used in front of a name: Captain John Smith, but not if used following a name: John Smith, captain. Or Judge Roy Bean, but Roy Bean, judge. There is one exception. When referring to the President of the United States, the word President is always capitalized. Some presidents of lesser organizations often feel the need to capitalize the term, but that is a matter of personal or company policy. Some also like to capitalize other major offices, like Governor or Associate Justice. This tendency reflects the belief that capital letters lend importance, but when and where to use them is optional.

Family members' names are capitalized unless the name is preceded by a possessive noun or pronoun. Aunt Jane handed Mom the flowers. But, my mom handed them back to my aunt.

Places

Geographical directions are capitalized only when referring to specific regions: the South that survived a war, the taming of the West. They are not capitalized when indicating direction: the team headed north to a stadium two blocks south of the border.

The entire company name of business organizations needs to be capitalized: ABC Company, The IBM Company. (Some firms insist on capitalizing The. Many don't.)

Countries are always capitalized, of course. So are the products that bear their names, such as French fry, Belgian waffle, Danish pastry. There was a time early in this century when people referred to all cars as Fords. A current trivia fad delves into the forgotten origins of some proper names attached to commonly used items. (Bet you've forgotten that there was a Mr. Ferris who invented the Ferris wheel or that there was a Frigidaire that preceded fridge.)

Things

Brand names are capitalized (Folgers, Plymouth, Macintosh) even when they become part of our language. Some companies make a point of insisting that the capital letter be retained in their names: Xerox, Kleenex, Sanka, Coca-Cola, for example. Use generic names—copier, tissue, decaffeinated coffee, cola—if you don't have the real thing. As usage of the proper names increases in our language, we tend to omit the capital letter (as in french fries and cheese danish).

Other commonly capitalized words include the days of the week,

months, and book titles. Tuesday, Saturday, June, and October are familiar. Books and other publication titles sometimes leave out capitalization
of certain words: conjunctions, articles and short prepositions. *The Rise
and Fall of the Roman Empire* demonstrates the uncapitalized conjunction, preposition and article. Always capitalize the first letter of titles. Be
careful not to capitalize *the* when it is not part of a proper title. (When the
Supreme Court meets . . .)

Names of study courses are capitalized only if they are derived from
proper names: French, Russian, but not biology, history. Names of specific courses are capitalized: Genetic Biology 101, Ancient History 202.

Seasons are capitalized only when they are personified, that is, given a
meaning that resembles people. When *Summer* smiles on us, we forget *Old
Man Winter*, haul out our *summer* shorts and put away our *spring* hats.

Historical events and historic eras are capitalized: the Dark Ages, the
Renaissance, the Days of Flower Power.

Always capitalize the first word of a sentence, the first word of a
salutation and close of a letter (Dear John, Sincerely yours), the first word
of a direct quote that is a complete sentence (She answered, "Of course, I
understand."), and the first word of a sentence fragment that substitutes
for a complete sentence (Such a shame!).

Whether or not you capitalize a.m. or P.M. is a personal choice unless
the company style manual says otherwise.

MAKING NOUNS PLURAL

If we had just one shot at providing a guideline to making plurals out of
nouns, it would be this: To make a noun plural, add a Simple *s* or *es*. But
then, Miss Miller wouldn't be earning her meager pay, would she?

Simple *S* or *ES* Endings

To make plural most nouns, add an *s*, unless the noun ends with *s*, *z*, *x*, *ch*
or *sh*, then add an *es*. Some people's names that end in these letters pose
strange problems of their own. Take the Ferris family, for instance. When
we write about all of them, we write *the Ferrises*. When we write about
their yard, we write *the Ferrises' yard*. Certain grammarians insist we add
's to produce any possessive, forcing us then to write *the Ferrises's yard*.
(Here is a good topic for debate.)

Ending in *Y*

If a noun ends in *y*, another problem arises. It becomes necessary to look at
the letter before the *y*. If the *y* is preceded by a vowel (*a, e, i, o, u*) add the
Simple *s* (keys, attorneys). If, however, the *y* is preceded by a consonant

(any other of the letters), change the *y* to *i* and add *es* (companies, secretaries, alimonies). Forget this guideline when pluralizing proper nouns (Kennedys, Gettys, Canarys).

Ending in *O*

If you want to open a real can of trouble, start making plurals of words that end in *o*. There are no rules, just exceptions. There seems to be no rhyme nor reason why some *o-* word plurals end in *s* and some in *es*. In fact, most dictionaries provide two plural forms for most of the words. That means that whichever you choose, either cargos or cargoes, you're right!

Here's some good news. Forget the option of inserting an e to make plurals of the *o*-words. When you find an *o*-word that requires a plural, revert to the Simple *s* guideline. Simplify your life. There is no reasonable explanation for using *s* on some words and *es* on others.

What you need is a good new dictionary. If you use any of these words often, check the dictionary, make your choice and be consistent.

Miscellaneous Plurals

After the trauma of words ending in *o*, you may be in a mood to approach the nouns that are made plural with few sensible patterns. Change the vowels to pluralize foot, goose, man, woman, tooth (feet, geese, men, women, teeth).

Some nouns require no changes at all to go from singular to plural: corps, deer, moose, sheep, series, species. They remain the same.

Only a couple of words fall into the category that requires *en* to make them plural: child (children) and ox (oxen). An archaic use of brother (brethren) is still used by some organizations.

There are a few words that change the *f* in a word to a *v* to make them plural: wife, wives; knife, knives; life, lives. Who knows why! Nor has anyone figured out why mouse turns to mice!

These Singular Nouns Look Plural

A few nouns that end in *s* are singular in meaning and require singular verbs: civics, economics, mathematics, news, phonetics, semantics, series. And some nouns end in *s* and may be either singular or plural in meaning, and are used only with plural verbs: goods, pliers, riches, scissors, thanks.

Compound Nouns

Compound nouns are combinations of two or more words that vary in plurals according to the components. If a compound word includes a noun combined with an adjective or preposition, the principal noun is made plural:

> fathers-in-law
> heirs-apparent
> lookers-on

If no part of the hyphenated compound word is a noun, the plural is added at the end:

> follow-ups
> strike-overs
> trade-ins
> write-ups

Likewise, if a compound noun is written without the hyphen, the plural is added at the end: businessmen, cupfuls, letterheads, stepchildren.

Latin Nouns Et Al

The American language is full of words brought in from other countries. Some estimate that more than 50 separate languages are incorporated into the language we use every day. Many of these words follow the guidelines above. A few stick with rules of their own language, especially Latin words.

Some Latin and Greek words that end in *is* are made plural by changing to *es*:

analysis	analyses
basis	bases
diagnosis	diagnoses

This has resulted in similar-sounding words treated in a similar way, like the ludicrous pronunciation sometimes given the plural for process. Although it is pluralized with a simple *es*, one often hears the plural mispronounced *process-eez*.

We use many Latin words that end with a plural *a*, which can be made singular by changing the *a* to *um*:

addenda	addendum
curricula	curriculum
data	datum
media	medium

Because the plurals end in *a*, we're tempted to consider them as singular. Constant usage of words like data and media are resulting in Americanization; that is, they are being used as both singular and plural in their original form, or as singular words utilizing the Simple *s* rule: datas and medias. (Note that medias are newspaper, radio and television, while mediums are people with special powers. Maybe they're not so different after all.)

What makes the adaptation of other languages to American intriguing is the application of gender in most Romance languages (Italian, French, Spanish). Nouns in those languages are given gender references, either masculine or feminine. There is no reason nor consistency of the application; they just are. When these words are incorporated into English/American, they may keep their gender attachments, at least for awhile.

The Latin plural rules are getting lost. Common usage in America is removing some of these nuances from our language. Until they are completely erased, you may want the guidelines. Here they are.

Latin words ending in *us* (masculine) are made plural by changing to *i*:

alumnus   alumni
nucleus   nuclei
stimulus   stimuli

Words ending in *a* (feminine) are made plural by changing to *ae*:

alumna   alumnae
formula   formulae
vertebra   vertebrae

Some grammar books and dictionaries are acknowledging such plurals as nucleuses, formulas, vertebras.

More Latin. Words ending in *ex* or *ix* have, until now, been made plural by changing to *ices*:

appendix   appendices
index   indices

Thankfully, that too is changing, allowing us to make the words plural by adding *es* (appendixes, indexes).

We're loosening up with the *on* words too, but in different ways. The singular criterion and phenomenon, made plural in the Latin by changing to *a* (criteria and phenomena), are finding acceptance today as criterias and phenomenons.

The French gave us the *eau* words, made plural by adding *x*. Now some of these words are given the Simple *s* ending to make them American plurals.

bureau	bureaus
trousseau	trousseaus

POSSESSIVES

When one thing belongs to another, our language has what is called a possessive form to express it. A possessive is formed by adding an apostrophe *s* ('s) or an apostrophe (') to the noun (the manager's report, the presidents' club). Considerable confusion encompasses using the possessive form of a noun, mostly because of the placement of the apostrophe. Here is a simple four-step guideline.

Step 1: Make certain that the possessive case is needed, that you aren't using a plural (they sometimes sound the same since they both can end in *s*).
The managers will report today. (not possessive)
The managers' report is due today. (possessive)

Step 2: Determine whether the noun is singular or plural.
The manager's reports are due today. (singular possessive—one manager)
The managers' reports are due today. (plural possessive—more than one manager)
If singular, go to Step 3.
If plural, go to Step 4.

Step 3: If singular, add an apostrophe *s*. See Step 2.
The manager's reports are due today. (singular possessive)
The man's timing is excellent. (singular possessive—one man)

Step 4: If plural and if it ends in *s*, add an apostrophe only.
If it ends in any other letter, add apostrophe *s*.
The managers' reports are due today. (plural possessive)
The men's timing is excellent. (plural possessive—more than one man)

For example: If you wish to form the possessive for the hat belonging to the lady.

Step 1: Belonging says it is possessive.
Step 2: Since there is only one lady, the noun is singular.
Step 3: Add an apostrophe *s* (lady's hat).

Another example: If you wish to form the possessive for hats belonging to all the ladies.

Step 1: Belonging says it is possessive.
Step 2: There now are several ladies (plural).
Step 3: Not singular.
Step 4: Since ladies ends in s, add an apostrophe (ladies' hats). If the hats belonged to men, we would have added an apostrophe *s* (men's hats).

Easy as 1-2-3-4. Conversely, when you see a possessive written, you can discern whether or not a single noun or a plural noun possessed the whatevers. The *witnesses' testimony* tells us immediately that more than one witness was testifying and they agreed on a single testimony.

Likewise, *the robber's alibis were all lies* says that only one robber made up a bunch of alibis.

VERBAL NOUNS

Sometimes words other than nouns behave like nouns. These words are called verbals. There are three of them—gerund, participle and infinitive—and they are discussed fully in Chapter 8.

For now, know that something called a gerund is actually a verb posing as a noun and must be treated as a noun. For instance, *to speak* is a verb. But when we use the gerund form *speaking*, it can behave as a noun, as in: Speaking exposes our thoughts.

The infinitive verbal involves the infinitive form of the verb (to do something) which also behaves like a noun. To function effectively is to set a good example. *To function* is the infinitive verbal.

Know also there is a participle, which is a verb posing as an adjective modifier. As in, a motivating impulse, or a motivated impulse. Both the words motivating and motivated are participles. (You can identify them by their base forms as verbs. Participles can lead us into all kinds of word entanglements that will be further clarified when we get to Chapter 8.)

But don't get entangled with verbals just yet. There's plenty of time to tackle these mind bogglers after reviewing verbs and all their idiosyncrasies.

NOUN AND VERB AGREEMENT

In sentences, nouns must agree with the verbs that tell about them. *When singular nouns are used, the singular verb form also must be used.*

The building sways in heavy winds.
The wind blows incessantly.

When plural nouns are used, the plural verb form must be used.

The buildings sway in heavy winds.
The winds blow incessantly.

A Helpful Note

Ironically, singular verbs often end in *s* (has, jumps, belongs) while plural nouns also end in *s* (members, kids, cars). One guideline that has helped people who struggle with this language: Imagine a shortage of the letter *s*. The *s* must be rationed out, one to a noun-verb combination. Either the noun or the verb gets it, not both.

Therefore: the members have . . . but the member has . . . In the same way, the kids jump and the kid jumps, and the car belongs and the cars belong.

Beware! This is not a hard and fast rule, just a guideline.

Consider subjects connected with *and* as plural.

When a subject is comprised of two or more nouns connected by *and*, treat them as a plural noun. That is, use the plural verb and plural pronouns. Consider subjects connected with *and* as plural.

The building and its occupants *sway* in any breeze.
The lights and the electrical equipment *are* threatened by storms.

There's an exception: when both words connected by *and* refer to the same thing (or person). Notice the use of modifiers *the* and *its* in the previous sentences, and the lack of a modifier in the following sentence.

The structural engineer and designer *is* always available when we need her.

Consider subjects connected with the word *or*, as singular (maybe).

Or gives you a choice of one or the other. Consider subjects connected with *or* as singular (usually).

The architect or engineer *needs* to decide on backup electricity.
The report or the cover letter, whichever is sent, *is* contained in its own envelope.

That seems to be easy enough. Two clues can verify what is going on: the number of the verb and the number of the pronoun. So we'll throw in a what if! What if one of the words is singular and one is plural and they're connected with or? Maybe this is easy too, once you remember what Miss Miller told you. Aha! You had forgotten. What she said was, "If you are faced with two subjects connected with *or*, one of them is singular and one is plural, *consider the word closest to the verb* when determining its number and when deciding which pronoun and verb to use. If one or the other sounds awkward, simply change the order of the subjects.

An artist's rendering or the *schematics are* sufficient to provide proof.
The schematics or the artist's *rendering is* sufficient to provide proof.
The location or the room *sites have their* own designated generator.
The inspector or the *engineers need* to see with *their* own eyes.

COLLECTIVE NOUNS

Some nouns seem to be plural, but may be used as a singular. These are called collectives and require a close look. Such words—group, team, company, board, jury, family, number—can represent either the individuals that make up the collective or the collective itself. Choose the verb form very carefully to express your meaning.

Both of the following sentences are correct, but they express different meanings.

The team have until Monday to choose uniforms.
The team has until Monday to choose uniforms.

In the first sentence, it is clear that each member of the team will have a say in the choice. In the second, the team will have to decide unanimously.

FINDING THE NOUN/VERB

To be sure the noun and verb agree, first you have to find them. In long sentences, this is not always apparent. Prepositional phrases often mess things up, separating the noun subject from the verb. Eliminate prepositional phrases when searching for the verb and its agreeable subject. Only the first two sentences that follow are correct.

The *board* of directors which meet on Tuesday of every other week and Thursdays in the summer months *is* made up of 12 people.
The board of directors is made up of 12 people.
The board of directors are made up of 12 people. (incorrect)

EXERCISES
(Answers to exercises are in the Appendix.)
Insert capital letters where appropriate:

1. an advertising agency in chicago is called syntax, inc.
2. the special clients of syntax are manufacturers in the city of chicago.
3. when the company president james valdez needed more help, he placed an ad in the wall street journal.
4. who knew the governor would seek a position as his communications director?
5. only one person at the agency knew that the governor was a friend of president valdez.

Change the indicated words to plurals.

6. The client *list* were divided between *attorney* and computer *company*.
7. The account *exec* often ate *tomato* in the board room using steak *knife*.
8. They discussed *datum* for the *write-up* contained in the file *index*.
9. This information helps *agency* provide the *medium* with better *analysis*.
10. The *client* considered the *process* as valuable *asset* to their *service*.

Where do the apostrophes belong in the following possessives?

11. Valdez birthday is tomorrow.
12. James mother is the founders sister.
13. There are three Jameses in Syntaxs company.
14. The new executive should be here in a weeks time.
15. Each ones anticipation must be kept in check.

Another challenge. The following is a personalized license plate. Does the driver have three sons? Or does the driver have a 3-year-old?

```
MYSONS3
```

2

The Handy Dandy Quick Pronoun Menu

PRONOUNS

One reminder that astonishes grownups is that pronouns represent nouns. Somewhere in what you're writing (or reading) is a noun that is being referred to by a pronoun, and it tends to be overlooked. A few pronouns may be exempt grammatically from that reminder (like somebody and anyone), but too often pronouns are used without regard to what they replace. The pronouns *they* and *it* are the big offenders. A Handy Dandy Quick Pronoun Menu is part of this chapter. It provides a hands-on review of pronouns to recall easily the proper use of pronouns. Subjects are found in Column A, objects in Column B, and possessives in Column C, a neat reminder that clears up a few mysteries. Compound pronouns, reflexive pronouns, and the agreement of pronoun and verb are discussed. A look at pronouns after comparisons and pronouns that follow *to be* are added, along with a few words about collective pronouns. Once and for all, the *who, whom* question will be settled, or will it?

To begin the subject of pronouns, you need to be reminded that pronouns substitute for nouns. They sit in where the noun is not repeated. Occasionally, we become careless and aren't sure just what the noun is. Writers often find that by getting a good sense of pronouns, writing becomes clearer and more direct.

Ever since learning about pronouns, you may have been foggy about just how many there are and what they do. Somehow you know that *I*, *me* and *my* are pronouns, but where do they fit in the scheme of the universe?

Be foggy no more! Below is a Handy Dandy Quick Pronoun Menu to clear things up for you. Before you look at the finished guide (at the end of the chapter), try to fill in the spaces by yourself.

	Column A Nominative The Do-er	Column B Objective The Do-ee	Column C Possessive The Owner
1st Person	_____	_____	_____
2nd Person	_____	_____	_____
3rd Person	_____	_____	_____

To begin, place all the first person pronouns in the first row across. First person means any pronoun relating to the person speaking, singular and plural: I, me, my/mine, we, us, our/ours.

Next, fill in the second row with second person pronouns; that is, pronouns relating to the person being spoken to, singular and plural: you, you, you, you, your/yours, your/yours. (This is the easy one. Please, do not include you-all, youse, yourn, or yez, even if your friends tell you that youse is singular and yez is plural!)

Finally, fill in the third row with third person pronouns, those relating to someone or something else: she, he, it, her, him, it, her/hers, his, its, their/theirs.

There you have it. To be certain you have the right pronoun in the right place, you can now refer to the end of this chapter. When we talk about subjects and objects (later on in Chapter 8), you'll be well-prepared.

Hold on, there are more pronouns than just those on the chart. You may even be surprised when you realize you already know them. You just don't often think of these words as pronouns. But they are.

And there are many more. Pronouns come in a variety of all-purpose styles, each with its own label.

Let's differentiate right off the bat. There are *personal and possessive pronouns* (the ones on the menu), *singular pronouns* (each, each other, all, some, anyone, who, nothing, either/neither, everything, much), a few *plural pronouns* (many, few, both, several, others), *reflexive pronouns* (personal pronouns with the word self or selves added), *relative pronouns* (who, which, that), and *demonstrative pronouns* (this, that, those and these). Using these labels, let's look separately at each set.

PERSONAL PRONOUNS

Personal pronouns are those listed in the Handy Dandy Guide. Anyone can see they are divided into three sets. Under Column A are the subject pronouns. These are the Do-er pronouns, the subject of the sentence or clause, the one that must agree with the verb. They include I, we, you (both singular and plural), he, she, it, and they.

Whenever using a Do-er pronoun, choose from Column A. These are the pronouns to look for in those up-until-now terrible instances when you need to answer the question, Who is it?

Now, you can respond confidently, It is I (you, he, she, it). In reviewing the stop-action verb *is* a bit later you'll learn that whatever lies on both sides of the verb must match. Because *it* is the subject. *I* also must use the subject form, that is, both *it* and *I* must come from Column A.

Also use Column A pronouns that follow the words *than* or *as* where another verb is implied. No one was better qualified than she (was). Both sons are taller than I (am).

Choose from Column A when the pronoun defines the subject and is set off with commas. This use is called an appositive since it makes positive that you know what you're talking about. Perhaps they should be called repeaters, since they repeat the subject in one form or another to clarify it.

> Two managers, *Gloria and I*, will lead the session. (*Gloria and I* are appositives of two managers.)
> The highest producers are the two district leaders, *you and she*. (*You and she* are appositives of two district leaders.)

The pronouns in Column B are the Do-ee pronouns. They are the ones used when you want to show who receives the verb from the subject. There are two ways this can be done, directly or indirectly.

Directly: They trained me for the job. (Who did they train? Me.)

Indirectly: He gives me the willies. The willies are what is given (the direct object), and the recipient is me (the indirect object). One test of the indirect object is to ask if something has been done to or for someone and that's the pronoun required (from Column B). He gives (to) me the willies.

Object also refers to use in prepositional phrases. Remember Miss Miller calling it the "object of the preposition"? *Don't give the credit to her*. To (preposition), her (object of the preposition). Therefore, we immediately recognize the need to go to Column B. Pronoun objects of prepositional phrases must come from the Do-ee column.

Perhaps this will forever remove the doubt from your mind about the words that follow *between*. Because *between* is a preposition, it takes an object (of the preposition). These always will be from Column B (me, us, you, her, him, it). At last, you know! There is no between I and she! All the following are okay.

Between you and me	Between you and him
Between you and her	Between her and him
Between him and me	Between her and me
Between them and us	Between them and me

Courtesy suggests that first person pronouns are placed at the end of a pronoun string, whether two or twenty. Between her, him, you and me.

Just like the Column A use of the appositive, or repeater, there is a Column B use of the appositive, that is making positive you know who is the object.

The best sales territory was given to them, Margot and him.
They never thanked their bosses, Jackson and me.

Perhaps now you won't revert to: Me and June went to the movies. Or, The doctor examined Harold and I. In the first sentence, the subjects should have come from Column A, June and I. In the second sentence, the objects of the doctor's examination should be chosen from Column B. Harold and me are the objects of the verb examined, answering the question, who was examined?

POSSESSIVE PRONOUNS

Column C deserves a section all its own, since the pronouns there are neither subject nor object. Rather, they are closer to adjectives. In other words, possessives show who something belongs to. This can be done in one of two ways. Either use the pronoun with the object owned (my book), or use just the possessive pronoun (mine). All of the pronouns except the first person end with the possessive *s*.
Note: pronoun possessives do not have apostrophes!

We can refer to my schedule as mine.
His opportunity was his alone.

gbonaccorso 15f3

Read 2021 ~~$~~

ReadTheory
password and
Username

Milwaukee Area Technical College

MILWAUKEE CAMPUS
700 West State Street
Milwaukee, Wisconsin 53233-1443
414-297-6600

Ramona looked at her desk calendar and knew that today was hers.
When Arthur forgot his appointment, he knew the blame was his.

Beware the Contraction

A puppy wags its tail. It's cute! (The apostrophe is used only for the
contraction of *it is* and never, never for the possessive.)
Theirs is not to wonder why.

Singular Pronouns

You may not have recognized them as pronouns in the past. However, they
are substitutes for nouns. Some function only as pronouns; some can also
function as adjectives. When they function as sentence subjects, they must
use a singular verb. More about pronoun-verb agreement later in this
chapter.

Some of the singular pronouns:

anybody	anyone	anything,	everybody
everyone	everything	somebody	someone
one	nobody	nothing	something
each	either	neither	much

Use them carefully. Often the subject pronoun is a long way from the
verb.

Each of the people in the accounting department on the third floor has a
parking space.
Somebody within the sound of my voice is about to be honored.
Either of the desks near the window is suitable for me.

Plural Pronouns

A few slightly disguised pronouns are plural and take plural verbs. Some
of the plural pronouns:

both	few	several
others	many	most

Many of the shopkeepers are rallying to stock the new persimmons.
A few of the fruit stands are unwilling to unpack them.
Several grocers have decided to pass on persimmons this year.

REFLEXIVE PRONOUNS

Nowhere in the Handy Dandy Guide is the word self. All the self words are called reflexives or emphatic pronouns: myself, herself, himself (never hisself), yourself, itself, themselves (never theirselves). There's a reason they are not included in the Guide. Their main purpose in our language is to add emphasis.

> I myself want to do the work.
> I want to do the work myself.

A secondary purpose is to act as an object of a verb or the object of a preposition.

> Mary gave herself time to prepare.
> He told himself never to repeat that mistake.
> Artemus and Magenta found the strength in themselves.

Notice that most of the self words in the first and second person come from the possessive Column C. The third person words come from Column B. Wouldn't you like to get your hands on the person who decided to switch to objects to cover her, him, it and them? There is absolutely no rhyme nor reason, no precedent, no logic. This is one you'll just have to remember.

Don't overdo the self pronouns. The simple pronoun usually is enough without the self.

> This company is operated by my children and myself. (No!)
> This company is operated by my children and me.
> I would believe a trusting person like yourself. (No!)
> I would believe a trusting person like you.

SINGULAR OR PLURAL

This isn't as difficult as it may seem!

Some pronouns can be either singular or plural, according to the meaning intended: all, none, any, more, most, some. The key is to look at the prepositional phrase (if there is one, and there usually is) that follows the pronoun in question. By reading the clues, you can determine whether or not the required verb should be singular or plural. This is one of those tight places where exact meaning can be transmitted by carefully choosing your words. Reading the work of a careful writer provides the clues to tell readers how many are being discussed.

Most of the good movies are disappearing. They are disappearing.
Most of the movie has concluded now. It has concluded.
All of the criticisms were unfounded. They were unfounded.
All of the criticism reduces the normal weekend audience. It reduces the audience.
None of the audience care if the lights are low. They don't care about lights.
None of the audience cares about salted popcorn. It cares about Milk Duds.

The pronouns *all* and *none* are up for grabs with some grammarians. (Since the experts can't agree, Miss Miller may just have skipped this part in her lesson plans.) It's really very simple. If the word clearly is meant as singular, it takes a singular verb, and the same for plurals. You, as writer or speaker, have the option to choose how many you're talking about and to say it that way.

None of the children is expected to leave the room during the movie.
All of the children are expected to be in their seats at 4 o'clock.
None are coming to see the newsreel.
All is not well in the mezzanine.

RELATIVE PRONOUNS: WHO, WHICH, THAT

Who/Whom

You knew you'd get to it. Probably one of the most nagging language problems is the decision to use *who* or *whom*. The news is good: current usage is moving away from the *whom*. Yes, we're dropping it from the language like we dropped *thee* and *thou*. Miss Miller probably wouldn't mind either, since it was difficult to teach.

There is a simple guideline that might help those who want to have the grammatical edge.

Place *who* in Column A, and *whom* in Column B (with *him* which also ends in *m*).

To test the choice when faced with the who/whom decision, look at the words that follow the who or whom.

Remove the who/whom and replace with either he/she or him/her, whichever makes sense. If he/she makes sense, you'll be correct to use who. (You have a subject from Column A.) If him/her makes sense, use whom. (You have an object from Column B.)

Try these guidelines on the following sentences:

Charles was the director (who/whom) we know could get the job done quickly.

(We know he could get the job done = who.)

(Whoever/whomever) said that Rita was a rising star?

(She said that Rita was a rising star = who.)

The argument is between Malcolm, (who/whom) loves chase scenes, and me.

(He loves chase scenes = who.)

She was the same co-star (who/whom) I would like to serve with.

(I would like to serve with her = whom.)

It is incumbent upon us to choose the actor (who/whom) we can rely on.

(We can rely on him = whom.)

On the same movie set is one more admonition. Be attentive about using *who* (in all its forms) only when referring to people. Use *which* when referring to things or animals. Use *that* to refer to things, animals and sometimes people (if referring to people as a type or class).

The leading actor was the one *who* was chased from the set.

The bull *which* is rambunctious was caught by animal rights activists.

It was the stage crew *that* sent the bull into the street.

Follow the same guidelines for *who*, *which*, and *what* when asking questions.

Who is that man I saw you with?

Which of the awards did you win?

What is the matter with a western film?

Now that you know the grammatical rule, you may use it when writing formally or when you want to let readers know that you understand the who/whom dilemma.

More often, however, you may want to opt for clear communication that doesn't sound affected or awkward. A simple solution might be to use *whom* only when preceded with the words *to* or *for*. The rest of the time, use *who*.

The school honored the family for whom it is named.

The head of the family, to whom they gave the award, spoke briefly.

The school honored the family who it is named for.

The head of the family, who they gave the award to, spoke briefly.

DEMONSTRATIVE PRONOUNS

If you can get a handle on *who* and *whom*, you will have no trouble extending the process to reach the right decision about *whoever* (subject) and *whomever* (object).

Tell whoever is shouting to leave the set.
You can ask whomever you wish to watch the day's shooting.

Related to the who/whom controversy, but not half as complex, is the use of *whose*. This word belongs in Column C; *whose* is the possessive form.

Whose name do you want on the credits?
Please give the script to Melody, whose desk is next to the door.

Warning! Warning! Do not use *whose* when you mean *who's*. There often is a mix-up between whose (possessive) and who's (the contraction for who is).
Who's the fellow whose left hand twitches during love scenes?

PRONOUN AND VERB COMPATIBILITY

Since you already know that verbs must agree in number with their subject, and you know that pronouns sometimes are the subject, here are a few tricks to make sure that verbs agree with pronouns that refer to specific nouns.

One business is . . Two businesses are . . One company is . . Two companies are . . That's easy.

A common mistake is to replace those nouns with pronouns that are plural. A company or a business is often considered as groups of people. The words, however, are singular. If we refer to a company or a business, we must use the pronoun *it*, not *them*.

The company held its annual meeting.
The business celebrated 35 years in business. It held an open house.

In the same way, be sure to treat proper company names as singular. The ABC Company *is* open for business. The Mainline Brothers, Inc. *is* celebrating *its* centennial. Don't be thrown by the plural-sounding name. The company is still one company.

Similar rules apply for other collective words: group, jury, team, audience, committee, council. In most usage, most of the time the words are singular and require singular verbs. The group meets, the jury decides, the team plays, the audience howls, the committee sits on its hands, the council disapproves.

However—you knew it was coming—there are times when these particular words need to act as plurals. And this wonderful language gives you, the speaker/writer, that option. So if the jury has been polled and is acting as individuals and you want to get that idea across, say: *The jury presented their verdict.* That clearly shows the listener/reader that you mean to consider the jury as individuals. To indicate the jury deliberating with a single thought, say: *The jury presented its verdict.*

The team played its heart out clearly says the team functioned like a unit. By changing that to *the team played their hearts out*, you can indicate that each member was doing their own job. (Hold on, you'll deal with the use of their in a few paragraphs.)

If you want to be even more precise to get across the idea of a group functioning as individuals, use a word like *number* or *member*.

Members of the jury delivered their verdict.
A number of the team played their hearts out.

These words require plural verbs and will leave no doubt about your meaning.

Note: When using the collective noun *number*, you can indicate the singular by using *the number* and the plural by using *a number*.

The number of members leaving the club is minimal.
A number of members are leaving the club.

Is this a wonderfully flexible language or what? You have the option of making a precise point by using specific endings. You can indicate diversity among members of a group or you can show cooperation with this simple choice. When you choose verb tenses, take care to say exactly what you mean.

COMPOUND PRONOUN SUBJECTS

Pronouns follow the same guidelines as nouns. If two or more pronouns are connected with *and*, they take a plural verb. If they're connected with *or*, they follow the guidelines described for nouns.

CAREFUL!

A pronoun usually is supposed to refer to a definite noun (person, place or thing). Take care to clearly transmit that connection.

The doctor and the patient went into *her* room. (Whose room did they enter?)

Ms. Goo and her agent, Ms. Adams, met with the director, but after an hour's discussion she couldn't reach a decision. (Who was undecided?)

After a session with the bookkeeper, the manager reported *he* didn't understand the regulation. (Who should be studying the regs?)

GENDER PRONOUNS

Look again at the Handy Dandy Guide. You'll notice that the only place where gender rears its head is in the third person singular. Not first or second, not third person plural, just third person singular. Does that give you a clue in eliminating sexist language from your business messages? Stay away from the third person singular unless you can identify the gender of the noun being reflected.

Pronouns should agree in gender with the nouns they replace.

Matson clearly is *her* own boss. (Matson is a woman.)

The new line supervisor, Barney Boston, didn't give us *his* Social Security number. (Barney is a man.)

The best thing to do for a rash is rub *it* with a lotion. (The rash is genderless.)

But what do you do when you're not sure of the gender, when the noun gender is not clear? Miss Miller told us to use the masculine *he/him* when you weren't sure of the gender.

If anyone needed the answers, *he* should ask.

Every reporter should have *his* own pad and pencil.

An artist needs to be careful with *his* paints.

These sentences imply that people needing answers are men; reporters are men; artists are men. Message like these, transmitted through using inappropriate masculine pronouns, are no longer acceptable. In a nonsexist society, these kinds of decisions are being eliminated. More and more people are opting for gender-free, inclusive language. Language users today can keep usage not only sexism-free but more accurate by using a variety of alternatives.

USING NONSEXIST LANGUAGE

While Chapter 21 deals with nonsexist usage, here are some easy ways to deal with the pronouns that give trouble. These are only a few ways that conscientious writers use to get around the third person singular sexist pronouns (he/she/him/her). Not all of the alternatives that follow can be used in every instance. Choose the one that best eliminates sexism and retains your intended meaning.

Recast the piece to use first or second person pronouns (I, we, you).

A sculptor uses the best clay he can find. (Excludes women as sculptors.)
As a sculptor, I use the best clay I can find. (First person)
As a sculptor, use the best clay you can find. (Second person)

Use third person plurals (they).
A craftsman chooses his tools from the Old Way. (Excludes women as artisans)
Crafters choose their tools from the Old Way. (Third person)

Even dare to use the third person plural pronoun with a singular noun antecedent.

Every pottery craftor may want to choose his own tools. (Sexist)
Every pottery craftor may want to choose their own tools. (Nonsexist)

Although a grammar purist may still grind their teeth over this usage, many notable writers have been using it for years, among them: Shakespeare, Hemingway, Shaw and Auden. It is the reasonable way to retain a sense of individuality while eliminating the implication that the individuals are men.

Use a clause instead of the pronouns to describe.

A frugal artist may choose to re-use canvases. (Excludes).
An artist who is frugal can re-use canvases.

Use genderless pronouns (one, everyone, each, all, none).

If an artisan works too long, he becomes burned out. (Sexist)
When working too long on art, one becomes burned out.

Eliminate the pronoun altogether.

An artist may select his paint colors from pastel or brilliant tones.
  (Sexist)

An artist may select paint colors from pastel or brilliant tones.

There are so many ways to write around sexist language, that there is no reason to offend anyone with words (See Chapter 21).

Anyone who needed the answers should ask.

Every reporter should have their own pad and pencil.

As an artist, you need to be careful with your paints.

Please, in the name of good language usage, avoid the awkward *his/her* or the overuse of the word *person*.

Pronouns Following *Be*

One more helping guide for using the correct pronoun. What case is used when a pronoun follows the verb *to be* or any of its forms (am, are, is, was, were, been, being)? This is the easy one. Use the pronouns in Column A, the subject form.

At the conference, the speakers were Martin and I.

We discovered the thief to be she.

If we had wanted a scapegoat, it could have been he.

The next president of the company will be she.

The most surprised people at the party were the hosts, he and I.

These sound uncomfortable, don't they? Want a simple way to check to see if you're using the right case? Reverse the sentence.

Martin and I were the speakers at the conference.

She was discovered to be the thief.

If we wanted a scapegoat, he could have been it.

She will be the next president of the company.

He and I, the hosts, were the most surprised people at the party.

After all, that's what was done with such awkward sentences in the first place; they were put together backwards.

Hints for Writers

With pronouns, try to remember to treat them like nouns; they are either subjects (Column A) or objects (Column B). Therefore, the rules that apply to verb and number agreement are the same for both nouns and pronouns. Not only will this keep you out of grammatical trouble, but you'll find it easier to say exactly what you mean.

If you want to be clearly understood, be careful about the little two-letter pronoun *it*. Notice how much you use the word. The search capability on a word processor will tell you how often you do. Ask yourself: Are you replacing a specific noun? Are you purposely avoiding a noun? Do you know what you're trying to say?

It occurred to me.
Some people like it.
It often happens that meetings run long.
It was a cold, dark stormy night.

Use your word skills to activate verbs and give your readers more action and more information.

What occurred to me was. . . .
Some people like eating out.
What happens is . . . *or* Meetings run long.
On a cold, dark stormy night. . . .

Another pronoun to avoid using without reason is *they*. Always know who you mean when you talk about *they*. Instead of:

They say the earth is cooling off.
After trying soup, they say it burns their tongues.
On television newscasts they promote their news specials.

Try something like:

Scientists agree the earth is cooling off.
Soup eaters say it burns their tongues.
Television newscasters promote their news specials.

Or:

On television newscasts, networks promote their news specials.

Too often writers overuse pronouns. Try leaving out the most useless. Love your pronouns. Treat them carefully. Use them efficiently.

THE HANDY DANDY PRONOUN GUIDE (COMPLETE)

	Column A Nominative The Do-er	Column B Objective The Do-ee	Column C Possessive The Owner
1st Person (sing.)	I	me	my, mine
1st Person (plural)	we	us	our, ours
2nd Person (sing.)	you	you	your, yours
2nd Person (plural)	you	you	yours, yours
3rd Person (sing.)	he, she, it	him, her, it	his/his, her/hers, its/its
3rd Person (plural)	they	them	their, theirs

EXERCISES
(Answers to exercises are in the Appendix.)

Select the best word.

1. (Whose/Who's) going to interview the new executive?
2. Let (he/him) who made the last decision do it again.
3. I think it was Elizabeth; (she/her) works in accounting.
4. I remember that James and (she/her) interviewed for two weeks.
5. Just between you and (I/me), it shouldn't take that long.
6. Among the four of (we/us), you'd think (we/us) could find a good executive.
7. Two staffers, Elizabeth and (I/me), will arrange the interviews.
8. "Give the job to (she/her)," Tony called from the Accounting Department.
9. He could have come over (himself/hisself) to tell us that.
10. "In fact, let (himself/him) take the job," Elizabeth suggested.
11. Everyone (has/have) the attitude of "Let somebody else (do/does) it."
12. James decided to do the job (himself/hisself); the task belonged to (he, him).
13. Several of the onlookers agreed, but I doubt that (he/they) will follow through.
14. At Syntax, Inc., few workers of the male gender (is/are) interested in kitchen work.
15. Many more than you think (is/are) turning up there lately, however.
16. At Syntax, you and (I/me) (is/are) going to get involved in decisions.

17. In this company (whoever/whomever) works for (it/them) makes (his/their) own coffee.
18. Neither you nor (she/her) (is/are) going to get into quarrels about it.
19. Let every (one/man/person) of (them/we/us) tell (themselves/himself/ourselves) that (they/we/us) will try to tell (their/our) own conscience to do what (they/we/us) feel is right.

3

Do/Be/Do/Be/Do

VERBS

The verb acts like a fulcrum in each sentence, balancing the other parts of speech. Every sentence needs a verb, whether or not it has anything else. A complete sentence has a subject and verb, even though the subject may be implied. Bottom line: every sentence contains a verb (or it's not a sentence).

Try not to get confused now; follow closely. We have action verbs and stop-action verbs. Action verbs show that something is going on and come in two flavors: active and passive. (With active, a subject does; with passive, the subject is done to.) The stop-action verbs simply show the status quo; nothing happens; the doing, without something being done to.

The variations of the stop-action verb *to be* are important to avoid if you want lively writing. To say that something is, doesn't tell much about it. Better to choose an active verb.

Verbs must agree with subjects. All verbs come with a full complement of tenses (present, past, future, perfect, simple, progressive and emphatic). Verb voices are the active and passive. Verbs also have moods (indicative, imperative, subjective), which may or may not change your life, but may provide some nuances in writing.

Verbs are the mainstay of good writing and deserve all the attention they get in this chapter and in Chapter 15. Whole books could be (and probably have been) written about verbs. There is so much to know. So much, that is, if you are a grammar teacher or a grammatical masochist. Imagine for a moment, if you can, a present participle subjective intransitive common copulative verb. You'd arrive at something like: *The instrument of torture would seem to have been causing intense pain*. Intense pain. Right.

Miss Miller would have a cow at the idea, but we're going to simplify verb usage. We won't even mention all those nasty words like aoristic, pluperfect, reflexive, intransitive, conjugation, and copulative—not unless we have to.

One of the problems in today's grammar is that each of us learned our grammar in different parts of the country, from different teachers, in different schools. The many, many labels applied to verbs are irrelevant (many have the same meanings, others are attached for no good reason except to make life difficult). What follows gives you a skeletal picture of verbs and their usage. By knowing this stuff, you'll have a better idea how to use verbs to form coherent sentences, you'll better understand another writer's (or speaker's) intent, and you could win big prizes on TV game shows.

Here, we'll call verbs as we see them, doing what they do best at the appropriate time. You can always look up Miss Miller if you want the fancy words. You probably won't have to, once you see how important verbs are. We already know that important things tend to be simple.

Important? In most languages, the verb is the chief requirement to form a sentence. Something has to happen, even if it is only to exist. That gives us our first clue to verbs. There are two primary kinds of verbs: action (the *do* words—something is happening) or stop-action (the *be* words— inactive, nothing going on, something just is).

ACTION VERBS

The action verbs usually show movement of the subject: jump, run, coalesce, immerse, drive, hear, throb.

The boy jumps the fence, searches the woods to find the place where two streams coalesce, in order to immerse his body, hot from driving a tractor all day and hearing the engine that throbs. Certainly, you can have more than one verb to a sentence. The boy (subject) is doing only some of these things; the streams coalesce; the engine throbs.

Compare the action verbs in that sentence to the existing (stop-action) kind of verbs. We could have written: The boy is hot; the stream is there; they seem to belong together. Nothing happens; they just are.

Action verbs (doing) may require an object (do-ee): The boy jumped *the fence*, searched *the woods*; the boy immersed *his body*, drove *a tractor* and heard *the engine*. (The emphasized words are the objects.) Or not: the boy jumps *down*, searches *for the streams*, drives *all day*, the engine throbs.

(The emphasized words are adverb modifiers, telling something about the verb.) These verbs do not require objects. They speak the action for themselves.

ACTIVE/PASSIVE VERBS

First of all, catch the difference between the words action and active. Action verbs are those requiring an object; we just discussed them.

Active and passive are the voices of the verb. That's all Miss Miller was talking about when she mentioned voices of verbs. Literally, the verb either speaks loudly or softly by this choice. Most action verbs can be either active or passive.

The active voice makes the subject of the sentence the do-er. The passive voice makes the subject the do-ee. It's that simple. When you want a strong, direct sentence, use the active. When you want to avoid the responsibility for who-dun-it, use the passive.

The chief exec opened the meeting. (Active—tells who did it.)
The meeting was opened by the chief exec. (Passive—turns the object meeting into the subject and the subject chief exec into the object.)
The meeting was opened. (Even more passive—avoids telling who did the opening.)

Some people thrive on direct confrontation and seldom slip into the passive. Some people use the passive all the time and find it difficult to write a direct sentence. What does that tell you?

Don't misunderstand; passive is not bad. There are times when you won't want to identify the do-er, purposefully and out of leniency.

A car is parked in my parking space. (passive)
Some jerk parked a car in my parking space. (active)

STOP-ACTION VERBS

Miss Miller had a variety of names for stop-action verbs: linking, intransitive, copulative. They all meant about the same thing. Instead of doing, these verbs just are.

Stop-action verbs that just exist sometimes are called linking verbs. Most of them are related to forms of to be: is, am, are, was, were, being, been. Many of them you may not recognize as being linking verbs. They tend to relate to the senses or a status: appear, look, smell, feel, taste, listen, sound, seem, grow, become, state, end; these are all linking verbs. Some of these sensible, stop-action verbs also can be action verbs (contain an object). Notice the difference of the same word used as both a stop-action and an action verb:

The executive *looks* important. (stop-action—important executive)
The executive *looks* daggers at the board. (action—daggers is the object; at the board, the indirect object).
The committee *smells* of onions and anchovies. (Whew! stop-action—of onions and anchovies describes the committee's odor)
The committee, meeting in the deli, *smells* the aroma of onions and anchovies in the kitchen. (action—the aroma is the object; of onions and anchovies modifies aroma; in the kitchen modifies smells)
The meeting *ended* in a deadlock. (stop-action—in a deadlock modifies the verb ended)
The chair *ended* the meeting. (action—the meeting is the object)

Stop-action verbs require no object. If there are words following the verb, they may modify the verb, or relate to the subject by describing or replacing the subject.

VERB MODIFIER (ADVERB)

The modifier after the stop-action verb describes the verb and is called an adverb. (The *ly* usually gives it away.)

She went willingly.
He drove carefully.
The meeting ended quietly.
The boy jumped down and searched frantically. (The adverb *down* tells where he jumped, and adverb *frantically* tells how he searched).

SUBJECT DESCRIPTION (ADJECTIVE)

Sometimes what follows is a word, phrase or clause that tells something about the subject, describing it and functioning as an adjective.

Everyone *seems* happy. (stop-action—happy modifies everyone)
The committee members *are* tired. (stop-action—tired describes the committee members)

The committee members *are* Harry, Samantha, Dolores, James and Orville. (stop-action—all those people replace the committee members and are known as appositives. An appositive clarifies or identifies the subject, that is, makes positive.)

SUBJECT REPLACEMENT

True linking verbs are stop-action verbs that are interchangeable with the subject. Picture the linking verb as an equal sign in a mathematical equation. Because they link what comes before and what comes after, such verbs are called linking and the sentences are usually reversible.

Happy (seemed) = everyone.
Tired (are) = the committee members.
Harry, Samantha, Dolores, James and Orville (are) = the committee members.

These words that further identify the subject, make positive, are sometimes called appositives.

Knowing the correct pronoun to use will come in handy in choosing the appropriate modifiers and appositives. When in doubt, check your dictionary and look for a verb's identification. Linking verbs are also called intransitive, noted in dictionaries as v.i., and copulative, which is a Ph.d. way of saying the verb connects the subject to a noun or pronoun or an adjective. Don't even repeat that, much less memorize it.

Eric decided. (The verb *decided* requires no object)
Eric spoke decisively. (The adverb *decisively* modifies the verb.)
Eric was decisive. (The adjective *decisive* modifies Eric.)
Eric decided the issue. (Active verb with an object, the issue.)

The first three sentences are stop-action; the last is action.

SOMETHING *IS* OR IT *IS*!

The little verb *is* (or any form of the verb *to be*) raises two options. In many foreign languages, especially Romance languages, two different words are used to distinguish between the two separate meanings. Americans have to make do with just one—*is*, or other forms of the verb *to be*.

The distinction has to do with forever. In one of those other languages, the speaker must first decide whether something *is* forever, or just *is* temporarily. Then the proper word must be chosen. In American, the *is* just is.

> She is a typist. (for today or for this year)
> She is a woman. (for all time, one hopes these days)
> He is happy. (back to today, temporarily)

Even though we don't have to make this distinction in the American language, you may want to be aware of the differences. Notice the use (and overuse) of the verb *to be*. One writer, a psychiatrist, managed to write an entire book without using the verb *to be* once. That is, he avoided labeling the subject for all time with the forever meaning, and he avoided making judgments with the temporary meaning.

Check your *ises* (that's the plural of *is*) from time to time to see if you're overusing the word in one context or another. Much of the time, a stronger action verb will power up your writing.

VERBS THAT DIDN'T START THAT WAY

In the previous sentence, the verb is *will power* and the word *up* is an adverb (where will it be powered?). Perhaps a better word would have been *empower*. In today's language, thanks to the computer industry and its technical language, one might be tempted to concoct a verb *uppower*.

Golly, this is a touchy subject. Miss Miller would faint at concocted verbs, such as: onload, offload, onturn, input, throughput, oversend, outgo, intake, even upchuck. But, listening to the speaking and writing world, these verbs are becoming more and more common. Weird, but common.

Segments of the business world (and other technical language units) love to coin words. While many words can be shaped into many forms, one faulty conclusion is that any word can be similarly re-shaped. This is a long way to explain how *prioritize* came into being. Miss Miller hates that word. It's a verb that grew out of a noun and is now included in most dictionaries.

> Managers need to prioritize their work each Monday morning.

Another relatively new business verb was derived from its noun form: source. Many business people now use *sourcing* as a verb to indicate the process of searching for a source.

The company will have to source more raw materials from adjacent areas.

Other new verbs of interest are *mirandize*, *blindside* and *gaslight*. Yes! These are understandable verbs in the American language. *Mirandize* means to read the Miranda Act rights to someone who is being arrested; *blindside* means to hit someone from their blind side; *gaslight* means to play with someone's head, to use psychopathic behavior like that depicted in the psycho-drama *Gaslight*. (You remember how Ingrid Bergman was mentally harassed by Charles Boyer?)

The officer *mirandized* the car thief.
The thief had tried to *blindside* the arresting officer.
She claimed he had *gaslighted* her by moving her belongings when she wasn't home.

Perhaps the best advice is to use words of this nature as you would technical language, carefully and appropriately. If your audience will understand what you're saying, go ahead.

SUBJECT-VERB AGREEMENT (THE *S* RATION)

Subject and verb must agree in number. Miss Miller said so.

If one person or thing is the do-er, then the verb must reflect the singular state. The same goes for the plurals. The hint about rationing the use of *s* (discussed in Chapter 1) applies equally to verbs.

Imagine there is a shortage of the letter *s*. You may use only one in a subject-verb twosome. If you use it on the subject, leave it out of the verb, and vice versa.

The position paper states clearly.
The position papers state clearly.

It's a simple test that won't apply all of the time, but it applies more often than you may have noticed.

The gold earring does things to your eyes.
The gold earrings do things to your eyes.
The chairs are out of place.
The chair is out of place.

The coffee machine was working yesterday.
The coffee machines were working yesterday.
Whenever the boss goes out of town, we play.
Whenever the bosses go out of town, we play.

DOUBLE VERBING

Double verbing is the tendency to use two or three verbs to say what you want. You may *try to imagine*, instead of *imagine*; or you may *make a decision*, rather than *decide*. Double verbing uses too many verbs.

> Today I thought I would sit down and begin to write to tell you what decisions I have made. (Count the verbs—five—count them!)

Try instead:

I'm writing to give you my decision.
The reasons I want to tell you what I have decided are many. (Too much)
My reasons are many for telling you my decision.

If you want to become identified with good clean writing, take a look at your verbs. Are you putting a strain on the verb pool? Are you using more than you need? Why is *making a decision* easier to write than *deciding*?

Over-verbing	Better
set up a schedule	schedule
start to print	print
begin to think	think
organize a plan	organize or plan
try an experiment	try or experiment
risk a change	risk or change

Over-writing with double verbs is one reason for long-winded reports. Don't fall into this trap.

WIMPY VERBING

Another trap to avoid is using wimpy verbs. While we have a rich language with more than a half million words, the public sticks to about 500 of them. This means two things: we aren't very creative with our language, and we apply multiple meanings to a few words. Some American words carry up to 100 meanings.

Consider the meaning of the following verbs: get, take, put, make, do, have, go, come. Look them up in the dictionary. Some of these words require pages to define. When a word carries so many meanings, it is difficult to know which one the writer has chosen.

The cure? Simple. Find exactly the meaning you wish and find a better word that carries your meaning. A good thesaurus provides enough alternatives for a lifetime. Make sure you have an updated copy of your own.

Put: place, drop, select, plunk down, prop up, file, locate.

Take: secure, acquire, grab, pull, receive, accept.

Verb Tense

Present Tense

The present tense shows something happening at this time. The tense can take the form of simple, ongoing or emphatic.

No, don't panic, we're not going to get into those complicated labels. This will be as painless as it possibly can be made. This is the meat of the verb discussion and may be all that you carried away from grade school grammar.

Verbs tell not only what happened, but when. The word *tense* refers to the when. It's the when that is under scrutiny now. We have three choices in time: past, present and future. To achieve this difficult feat, we must enter the contest with a clear head, keen eye, sense of humor, and sometimes engage the assistance of auxiliary verbs, such as *has*, *be*, *can*, *will*.

In some Eastern languages, there is just one verb. To make it past tense, they add the words that indicate when it happened; to make it future, they add words that indicate when it will happen. Verb: to wave. I wave yesterday. I wave today. I wave tomorrow. Too easy! Some Native American tribes had a better idea. They just used the verb they wanted and pointed over their shoulder for past tense, to the ground for present, or to the horizon for future.

In this country, we like to make life difficult with complex mechanisms. And we like to label them. Knowing those labels in grammar isn't as important as knowing that they exist and knowing how they participate in our language.

Three forms are offered on the menu in the present tense of a verb: simple, ongoing and emphatic. They simply are degrees of using the present tense.

Simple:

Simple: I shout.
Progressive: I am shouting (ongoing action).
Emphatic: I do shout (you bet your life I do!).

By adding auxiliary verbs, you can form the perfect or completed tense.

I have shouted.
I have been shouting.

Stick with it; there's more. The following sentences are simple present tense sentences.

You do your best.
She catches your cold.
He takes two hours for lunch.

Ongoing:

Another form of present tense is the *present ongoing*. Sometimes this form is called a participle. (Ooh, we weren't going to use that word just yet.) Sometimes the way to recognize this verb is the use of *ing* or *ed* with an auxiliary verb in front.

You are doing your best.
She is catching your cold.
He is taking two hours for lunch.

To make verbs perfect (that is, completed) use the present tense with the auxiliary verbs *has*, *has been*, *have*, *have been*. This tense shows that something has just been completed, that some action begun in the past may continue into the future, and that past actions may happen again.

You have been doing your best. You have done your best.
She has been catching your cold for the past few days. She has caught your cold and will suffer for weeks.
He has been taking two hours for lunch since he started to work here. He has taken two hours for lunch and doesn't think a thing of it.

Past Tense

The *simple past* indicates action that happened completely before the present time and may be formed by either regular or irregular verbs. (See above.) You should have no trouble with:

You did your best.
She caught your cold.
He took two hours for lunch.

Past complete requires an auxiliary verb (had, had been). This tense indicates an action that occurred before a past time or prior to another past action. The implication may be in the verb or it may be spelled out.

You had done your best.
You had done your best but she did better.
She had caught your cold.
She had caught your cold before you kissed her.
He had taken two hours for lunch.
He had taken two hours for lunch before anyone noticed.

Future Tense

The *future* tense is formed by adding the auxiliary *will* to the present tense.

You will do your best.
She will catch your cold.
He will take two hours for lunch.

The *future complete* tense uses the auxiliaries *will have* and *will have been* to indicate an action completed by a specified future moment or prior to another future action.

You will have done your best (by completing the training program).
She will have caught your cold (after another long kiss).
He will have taken two hours for lunch (in another half hour).

Progressive Tense

The progressive tense indicates action that is ongoing, progressing nicely, thank you. It is formed by adding the corresponding time tense of the auxiliary verb *to be*.

Present progressive: You are doing your best.
Past progressive: She was catching your cold.
Future progressive: He will be taking two hours for lunch.

Emphatic/Intensive Tense

One more little tense and then we're through. The intensive tense is used when you want to get intense about something that is happening or has happened. To accomplish this, add the appropriate word form of *do* to the verb in the present tense and vavoom! the emphatic.

> Present intense: He *does take* two hours for lunch.
> You *do do* your best.
> She *does catch* your cold.
> Past intense: She *did catch* your cold.
> You *did do* your best.
> She *did catch* your cold.

SPLIT INFINITIVES

This doesn't bother us now as much as it used to bother Miss Miller. She warned often about placing words between the words *to* and the verb of the infinitive (to be, to shine, to draw). Within reason, don't let this old rule bother you. The following are perfectly clear as to meaning.

> She wanted to never be in the office after dark.
> If you want the sun to always shine, go to Panama.

But try to avoid the big split (in long sentences). The following is a wide open ravine of a split infinitive:

> Anyone wishing to as a convenience because of the upcoming holiday draw their paycheck early may do so.

SPLIT VERBS

When using auxiliary verbs or two-part verbs, the natural inclination is to toss an adverb in the middle. Go ahead.

> He will always have our allegiance.
> We had never been so happy.

Just make sure the adverb is actually where you want it. Many feel the adverb should be placed before or after the entire verb.

> He always will have our allegiance.
> We never had been so happy.

Watch out when using the infinitives; they can be awkward with that split.

She wanted not to ever see him again. (Awkward)
She wanted not ever to see him again. (Better)

In general, try to keep the verbs together, especially when too many intervening words could mess up the sentence.

She too could have gone.
She could too have gone.
She could have gone too.

To sometimes split a verb is not as bad as to often or with many words and clauses in the intervening space like this split an infinitive.
Enough said.

REGULAR AND IRREGULAR VERBS

Remember the long lists of verbs that Miss Miller made you memorize? Some of the kids giggled at drink-drank-drunk. The list (most likely longer) may have looked something like this:

Present	Past	Past Participle
catch	caught	caught
do	done	done
drive	drove	driven
go	went	gone
lead	led	led
ride	rode	ridden
swim	swam	swum
take	took	taken

What you notice is that none of the past tense verbs end in *ed*. That's because none of the above are regular verbs. Regular verbs form the past tense by adding *ed*.

I walked all the way home.
We talked until the break of day.

Verbs that show up on the lists are called irregular verbs. They have to be memorized, verb for verb, or looked up in the dictionary every time you use one of them. There are no guidelines for irregulars.

For most American verbs, the present tense is found in the basic word which is given as an infinitive (*to* before the verb). When you're scouring a dictionary, you'll notice that some verbs have some of this stuff after them:

    go v. went, gone, going
    run v. ran, run, running

This information is what shows up on the memorized lists of irregular verbs.

Why the past participle? And why do some dictionaries add the participle? No comment. We're trying to stay away from the *p* word here. One would reason that the third column should be the future tense, but dictionary writers don't buy that.

Participles are odd verbs, individualists, renegades. They have lives all their own.

TIME OUT

A participle is a word that can participate as both a verb and an adjective. As a verb it can take an object or not. It can happen anytime, past, present or future. For discussion of the participle behaving like an adjective, see Chapter 8.

Warning: A few verbs are both regular and irregular. What determines their regularity depends on how they are meant. Take, for instance, the verb *to fly*. It can mean either to fly out with a long baseball drive (irregular), or to fly like the baseball (regular). The past tense of the former would be flied; the past tense of the latter would be flew.

    The third hitter in a row flied out to center field.
    The ball flew like a bird into the grandstand.

Here's another that can go either way: to shine. The regular verb is used to mean polish; the irregular refers to glow.

    (Regular) The pitcher shined his mitt until it glistened.
    (Irregular) The pitcher's mitt practically shone in the dark.

Dictionaries are pretty good about telling you that a verb can go either way. They give two past participles (shine v. shined or shone). However, many dictionaries don't show usage and leave the reader hanging as to when to use which participle. Maybe this is why many people who are trying to pick up American have trouble. (It is also one of the reasons anyone speaking American has trouble.)

MOODS

Verbs come not only in tenses and voices, but in moods. These correspond to the way we feel, similar to the emotional emphasis available when we speak. Generally, we recognize three moods: the plain, the demanding, and the Fairy Tale Syndrome.

The Plain Mood

This is the usual mood used for a normal kind of statement or question. Teachers would call it the indicative mood, but you can ignore that and call it plain.

The company enjoys parties any time of the year.

The Demanding Mood

The demanding mood is the one that gives the orders. (Teachers call it the imperative.) Alter your mood and take a swing at it. Simply remove the subject of a plain present tense sentence and imply *you*. Demands can be softened with a please in front or behind. Occasionally, you'll want to add an exclamation mark.

Enjoy parties any time of the year.
Stop it!
Get a move on.
Please be in my office at eight in the morning.

The Fairy Tale Syndrome

Teachers call this by a formidable word, subjunctive, meaning lacking in reality. What it refers to is actually the Fairy Tale Syndrome. *If I were a rich man*, could be such a mood. It refers to something that is not possible. If the possibility exists, the sentence would read: *If I was a rich man*.

If I am a rich man, tell me how much I am worth. This is a plain, ordinary sentence that ought to read: *If you think I am a rich man*.

The old subjunctive is disappearing as language usage becomes modified and simplified. Current business usage recognizes it only as a wish mood.

If he were ten years younger, he'd win the match easily. (He can't be ten years younger.)

If they were here now, they would agree. (They aren't here.)

What makes this worthy of discussion is the use of *were* in what amounts to the present tense. The present tense is usually *is* or *are*. Using the present tense may alter the meaning of the sentence.

If he is ten years younger, he wouldn't be gray. (He might be ten years younger than he admits.)

If they are here now, let them speak. (They might be here.)

Both of the above sentences don't imply the absence of fact.

But look what happens when the actual past tense is used: *If they were here yesterday. . . .* A whole new ball game, isn't it? To indicate the past tense in the Fairy Tale mood, throw in the auxiliary verbs *would have been. If they would have been here yesterday . . .*

There's more. First, let's complete the sentence.

If they *would have been* here yesterday, this problem *would have been* eliminated.

Two *would have beens* get a bit awkward. Leave one of them out. Use the simpler past tense in either the clause or the main sentence, but not in both.

If they had been here yesterday, this problem would have been eliminated.

If they would have been here yesterday, this problem would be eliminated.

Another use of the Fairy Tale mood is the future tense, something that you are hoping, suggesting, requesting or demanding to happen. This one requires the use of the verb *be*.

I am recommending that all vacations *be* lengthened.

She requested that everyone *be* on time.

My wish is to *be* elected mayor.

We demanded the troublemakers *be* removed from the room.

While the above sentences are appropriate, in most business usage, the *be* gets overworked. It is often used when a simple tense verb would do.

If Ted be playing games, he be in trouble. (No!)
If Ted is playing games, he is in trouble.
Whether these fans be in the stands or on the court, they love the game.
    (No)
Whether these fans are in the stands or on the court, they love the game.
    (Better)

The best news is that the subjunctive is losing ground in our language usage. Perhaps the safest way to handle the Fairy Tale Syndrome is to use *was* if you mean it and *were* if you're using wishful thinking.

If I was President.
If I were President.

Which meaning fits closest to your aspirations?

SHALL OR WILL?

There was a time when the distinction between these two words drove grade schoolers wild. Maybe you remember the trouble between these choices.

Today you can relax. The shadowy nuances have been dropped in all but the legal or legal-like forms of usage. Use *will* to your heart's content.

And when you get serious and want to startle someone into complying with your request, toss in the *shall* and duck. This serves as a warning or admonition that you mean business.

There shall be no smoking in this office.
All employees shall use the back door when arriving at and leaving
    work.

The ironic part of this guideline is that the message would probably get across without shall.

There will be no smoking in this office.
All employees will use the back door when arriving at and leaving
    work.

When the message comes from on high or is delivered in a memo in a plain brown envelope, we tend to take it seriously.

LIE/LAY

Perhaps we can lay the matter of lie and lay to rest; let it lie in peace.

Most of us can remember "Now I lay me down to sleep." Let this be a help to remember that lay is an action verb that takes an object. You have to lay something. In the case of the prayer, it is me. I am laying myself down to sleep.

Lie, on the other hand, takes no object. It simply lies there. (The old stop-action verb.)

Our problems with these words rest in the past and participle forms of the words.

Lay (present), laid (past), have laid (past participle), laying (present participle). *Lay* means to set, to place or put something. There has to be a something to put.

Lie (present), lay (past), lain (past participle), lying (present participle). Lie means to recline, to rest in a reclining position. Something can't do much just lying there. Aha, you noticed that the past tense of *lie* is *lay*, the same as the present tense of *lay*. This is the trouble spot.

Present	Past	Past Participle	Present Participle
lay	laid	have laid	laying
lie	lay	lain	lying

I said I would *lay* the report on your desk in the morning.
I *laid* it there this morning where it *lay* all day.

Those past tenses are the ones that give us the trouble. It may help to memorize them.

Then there is the other *lie*, the verb that means to tell a fib. This *lie* is a regular verb that takes regular endings: lie, lied, lying.

EXERCISES
(Answers to exercises are in the Appendix.)

1. Using the following statement, write three sentences in each of the three basic simple tenses (present, past, future):

     The president (to hold) interviews in the cafeteria.

2. Use the appropriate form to turn the above statement into past perfect and future perfect tenses.

3. Now turn it into present, past and future ongoing forms.

4. How about changing it into present and past intensive? Do it.

5. Change your mood and become imperative (demanding). Make it that kind of verb!

6. Turn the verb into a subjunctive. Re-write the sentence and give it a shot both ways: wishing and stating.

7. Repeat the above exercises with the following sentences:
   a. The Wall Street Journal ad (to evoke) all kinds of responses.
   b. James (to interview) thirty-two prospects.
   c. The entire staff (to play) the games involved in greeting a new associate.

8. Change this sentence to unsplit the infinitive(s):

   Whatever is needed to forever and ever until the end of time keep this office operating is to absolutely and as quickly as possible be done.

9. Select the best verb form in the following:

It is evident that Tony (can/could) learn to manage a department.
I managed to jam the copier that the repairer (has/had) just fixed.
What (is/was) the name of the guy who is our copier rep?
How many people would you guess (worked/work) in this company?
We never mention the good reports Elizabeth (writes/wrote).

10. Select the appropriate tense for the verbs in the following sentences. Keep them simple and active (no passive, intensive or progressive):
   a. By the time the interviews were over, James (to lose) his voice. (past perfect)
   b. The candidates often (to speak) little during an interview. (future perfect)
   c. In another two weeks, the firm (to announce) its new account executive. (future perfect)
   d. You (to prepare) the evaluation of the candidates for the Board. (three ways: past/future/imperative)
   e. The printout (to display) the qualifications of the winning candidate. (future)

11. Change the following passive sentences into active:

The qualifications were delivered to the Board before the meeting.
Voting procedures are explained to the Board by James Valdez.
Qualifications were read aloud by Valdez.
Recommendations of the finance officer were made to the Board follow-
    ing the reading.

12. Write a sentence to use each of the indicated verbs below:

control (past perfect)
drive (present perfect)
honor (present participle)
create (future)
listen (future perfect)
develop (past)
fill (infinitive)
change (imperative)

4

Tell About It

ALL-SIZE ADJECTIVES

Adjectives modify nouns and pronouns. In this chapter you'll find discussions about possessive adjectives, comparatives, ultimates, adjective clauses and phrases. You may be surprised at the impact of specific adjectives vs. non-specific; and you may chuckle at the misplaced adjectives (always put the modifier close to the modified). And did you realize that articles—a, an, the—are types of adjectives? Some adjectives deserve very special attention—only, almost, all—while others are just plain confusing: almost or nearly? continual or continuous? likely, liable, or apt? And why not use lots? And whatever could be wrong with a nice word like nice?

The prettiest, ugliest, strongest, weakest words are adjectives. They're the words that dress up (or down) nouns. Look into her clear, blue eyes. Run your fingers through his curly, brown hair. You can use adjectives sparingly, one or two at a time, or you can use whole strings of them. The gentle, straightforward, whispered, resonant voice had its lethargic, somnolent effect on the disorderly, confused, riotous, deranged crowd.

Sometimes it takes a whole phrase to describe a noun. My home, the last one on the block, is easy to find. If you want a fancy label, unsurprisingly, this is an adjectival phrase.

In short, adjectives (words, phrases, clauses) modify (describe, limit or restrict) nouns. They generally answer the questions: What kind? How many? Which one? They paint pictures with descriptive words that give your writing greater depth and meaning. And they generally are found in front of the noun. When you want to make a point of some adjective, place it after the noun. (The voice, gentle and resonant, calmed the crowd, disorderly and riotous.)

Another place to look for adjectives is following a stop-action linking verb, especially that little *is* word. Jerry is tall; Jerry is happy; Jerry is nuts. Tall, happy, nuts. Yup. That pretty well describes Jerry. These (for the label seekers) are called subject complements. They complement (describe) the subject.

Adjectives seem to bring us closer to people through language, make us notice and feel more of what we're talking about. For instance, you have a briefcase, eyes, and a jacket. Add an adjective, let's say *blue* to each. Now you have a blue briefcase, blue eyes, and a blue jacket. The things become visible; there is more to notice.

To become even closer, make the adjectives judgments. Try inserting one of these adjectives: pretty, large, baggy, sleazy. Get the idea? Now you're getting personal!

Business executives and sales people use adjectives in much the same way as advertising copy writers. Some use them to describe accurately; others overuse them. Notice how skillfully adjectives can shape ideas, opinions, even appetites. What appeals to you more: a hamburger or a sizzling, juicy, onion-seasoned hamburger? For a lesson on adjectives, read the menu in a good restaurant.

POSSESSIVE ADJECTIVES

Just let somebody own something and they'll adjective it to death. My house, my briefcase. The same with their office, her desk, his golf clubs. These are called possessive adjectives and combine the elements of Column C (Chapter 2) with the noun possessed.

Nouns also can be used as possessive adjectives: Alfred's briefcase, the president's desk, Priscilla's golf clubs. Alfred, the president, and Priscilla have become adjectives. The same applies to: the team's loss, the car's engine. However, try to stay away from inanimate things owning other things. Better to change that to the engine of the car.

And if you're wondering, yes, the articles—the, a, an—are also considered adjectives. The only place they can cause trouble is when *a* and *an* are used before words that begin with vowels or silent consonants. Your ears should tell you which one to use. The *a* is used in front of hard sounds: a machine, a year, a hallway, a unit, a uniform. Hey, you noticed! Those last two are vowels. Yes, but they don't sound like vowels. The vowel *u*, because of its ee-ew sound, calls for the article *a*. Furthermore, notice that the sometimes-vowel *y* also requires the article *a* (a yak, a yuck, a yoke).

Use *an* in front of nouns beginning with vowels or soft consonants: an ear, an abstract, an opinion, an upper deck, an hour, an honor.

But what if you have two nouns in a row, one that starts with a consonant and one with a vowel? The rules tell us to use both articles, although most of us get by with only one.

They want to choose a lawyer and an accountant.

If you want one person to handle both those roles, then use one article: *They want to choose a lawyer and accountant* (one person with two professions). This is one of those occasions when knowing the guideline could make an impression on someone (who had the rule drummed in back in grade school). Most people wouldn't notice, but you—and they—will now.

Good writers select adjectives carefully. They can be overdone, or rather over-used. (See how it works? *Overdone* would best be used only with a barbecue.) Using specific adjectives to define specific nouns spices up writing, makes it come alive. It also often pins down responsibility.

Tell your readers exactly how many? two hundred people; what kind? overdrawn accounts; which one? that new First Bank savings program. You can change the bland: *People had accounts in the program.* Into the specific: *Two hundred people had overdrawn accounts in that new First Bank savings program.*

The Only One

The adjective *only* offers the opportunity to talk about placing modifiers close to the words they modify. Try placing the word *only* in different places in the following sentence:

She had time for me.
Only she had time for me.
She *only* had time for me.
She had *only* time for me.
She had time *only* for me.
She had time for *only* me.
She had time for me *only.*

The same exercise works with most modifiers. Place them in the wrong spot and they can discombobulate the entire idea. They can cause havoc in some cases. Phrases are notable for doing that.

The man entered the office only claiming to be the patient of Dr. Roger's who was sexually dysfunctional. (Who had the problem?)

EVEN

Even is another adjective that can change the meaning of a sentence by its placement. Great care must be given to place the modifier next to the word it modifies. The word has several meanings: flat, smooth, tranquil, uniform, equal in degree. (As an adverb, *even* means: to a higher degree, at the same time, in spite of, in fact.)

Insert the modifier *even* in the following sentence and select the meaning from those just given.

The band leader insisted that the 76 trombones be better synchronized.
Even the band leader insisted that the 76 trombones be better synchronized. (adjective)
The band leader *even* insisted that the 76 trombones be better synchronized. (adverb)
The band leader insisted *even* the 76 trombones be better synchronized. (adjective)
The band leader insisted that the 76 trombones be *even* better synchronized. (adverb)

QUANTITY/NUMBERS

Adjectives indicating quantity or number need to be considered carefully. *This*, *that*, *those* and *these* are Column A pronouns which can serve as adjectives when modifying specific nouns or other pronouns. This dish, those cars. Beware of sneaky nouns that have questionable states of singleness. Use *this sort* or *that type*, and *these sorts*, *those types*. Also, *this company*, *that team*, *these companies*, *those teams*. And please, oh please, don't snitch from Column B and choose *them* as an adjective.

Don't ever choose them (Column B) pronouns! (Ugh!)

Words like *few*, *many*, *some*, *all*, *any* need mention here. They can be used either as adjectives when they modify other words, or as pronouns when they stand alone.

Few people realize the importance of exercise. (adjective)
Few chose to read the game rules. (pronoun)
Any one of the team could have scored. (adjective)
Any is able to hit a home run. (pronoun; note that *any* is singular and takes a singular verb)

Comparative Adjectives

> *"Good, better, best;*
> *Never let it rest*
> *Until the good is better*
> *And the better best."*

Thank you, Miss Miller. Jingles like these make remembering easier. Adjectives are great for comparing. This is better than that; she is the richest of her classmates; the meeting was longer than Monday's. Ordinarily, we can simply add *er* to an adjective to produce the comparative (of two things) or *est* to produce the superlative (of three or more things).

The rule says you can do this with adjectives of one or two syllables, but with longer adjectives, use one of the following words: more, most, less or least. Following the rule would result in words like funner, funnest, hurtfuler, hurtfullest. (Our language has changed so that we can refer to someone as a fun person and mean something different than a funny person. Ah rules!) One guideline suggests the use of *more* and *most* with the long adjectives. You decide how long.

For the most part, this guideline can be followed. But treat it carefully.

Base adjective	Comparative	Superlative
pretty	prettier	prettiest
sorry	sorrier	sorriest (watch the spelling)
long	longer	longest
capable	more capable	most capable
detrimental	more detrimental	most detrimental

A few adjectives qualify as irregulars. Good, better, best; bad, worse, worst; little, less, least; much, more, most.

The little adjective *far* has another problem. It has two choices for comparative and superlative forms—farther/farthest or further/furthest.

Handy Hint: Remove the far out of farther and use farther and farthest only when distance is concerned. When you reach abstracts or extent, switch to further and furthest. Further has to do with the concept of more. (Forget the logic that would have its positive form as *fur*!)

It is a *far* better thing that we do. (base adjective)
You will travel *farther* with a bike. (comparative)
The *farthest* you could travel is 20 miles a day. (superlative)

Taking this one step *further*, a car is faster. (comparative)

That is the *furthest* level of efficiency for physical health. (superlative)

The team *furthered* their health program by walking *farther* every day.

ULTIMATES

Beware that some words cannot be compared and cannot take modifiers. They are called ultimates. Like being pregnant, there are no degrees. One cannot be somewhat pregnant, a bit pregnant. Likewise, one cannot be somewhat unique or very unique.

Several words fall into this category, but need to be considered in context with their use. For instance, perfect. There is no degree of perfection as very perfect, somewhat perfect. However, it would seem perfectly all right to talk about seeking perfection and use words like nearly perfect.

When Mary Poppins described herself as practically perfect, she was not indicating a degree of perfection (as if she had used *nearly*). She was indicating she was perfect in a practical way. Practically is an adverb (the *ly* says so!)

By using a modifier such as the adverbs *nearly*, *very*, *almost* with an ultimate, it is possible to indicate the attempt to become the ultimate. Just know what you're handling when you try it. There actually could be a state of being nearly pregnant, very round, almost last, the very best.

Some other ultimate words are: first, only, round, correct, dark, light, silent. Perk up your attention when you dabble with these words. They could rear back and snap at you.

COMPOUND ADJECTIVES

In our language, combinations of two or more words are used to describe. The combinations serve as single adjectives and must be connected with a hyphen. For instance, run-on sentence, nose-to-the-grindstone worker, I-don't-care attitude, brown-bag lunch. Adjectives so constructed are excellent tools for describing precisely what a writer chooses to say.

Of course there are hitches. The words need each other to make sense. If you wanted to indicate a short, incomplete report, you can get by with the comma. Both short and incomplete are adjectives in their own right. But if you talk about a long-term, overly-complex contract, you need the hyphens. We did not mean either a long contract or a term contract, but a long-term contract. What happens is appropriation magic. Nouns, adverbs, pronouns, even verbs are borrowed to describe—magically turning themselves into adjectives.

When you later refer to the contract running for a long term, do not use a hyphen, because now term is the noun and long is its adjective modifier. Only the hyphens can do the magic. Notice that hyphenated words usually precede the noun modified. When the words are used after the subject noun, the hyphen is not needed.

The all-night jazz bar is on Second Avenue.
The jazz bar on Second Avenue is open all night.
The hard-to-please audience sat on its hands.
The audience was hard to please.

Other hyphenated words always require the hyphen (numbers such as *thirty-five* and fractions such as *one-half* and specially *con-structured* words). We'll talk about them in Chapters 13, 17, and 18.

If you choose to use an adverb as part of your adjective description, you won't need the hyphen. For instance: the *fully cooked dinner* or the *dangerously overloaded computer.* The adverb (ending in *ly*) is clearly the modifier of the adjective that follows. More about that when we get to Chapter 5.

You can also leave out the hyphen when using compound nouns that are easily recognized: third grade teacher, special delivery letter, string bean casserole, North Dakota winter, New Deal economics.

To insert the hyphens in the right place in the following requires more information. Where would you put them?

On sale are three quarter pound steaks. (Three quarter-pounders? or three-quarter pounders?)
The insurance company occupies twenty three room suites. (How large are the suites? Three or 23 rooms?)
Please sell me 50 gross boxes of ballpoint pens. (Do I require 50-gross boxes or 50 (one) gross boxes?)

ADJECTIVE PHRASES/CLAUSES

There are times when one word or two just won't do it. An entire phrase or clause is needed to get the descriptive point across. (You remember the difference between a phrase and a clause. The clause includes a verb; the phrase doesn't. Of course you remember!)

An adjective phrase describes a noun or pronoun, exactly as a single-word adjective does.

The committee on aviation planned the new airport.

The phrase *on aviation* modifies committee. When such a modifier contains a verb, it becomes a modifying clause, as in:

The committee to study aviation planned the new airport.

Since *to study* is a verb. Well, you see what is meant.
Again, placing the modifier close to the word modified can eliminate some unusual mistakes. Consider:

Look at the woman standing next to the horse's hat.

When is meant: Look at the hat of the woman standing next to the horse.
The placement of commas in a sentence containing an adjective phrase or clause can change the entire meaning.

The company office which is in Paris employs 12 people.
The company office, which is in Paris, employs 12 people.

In the first sentence, the company may have several offices, and we're talking about the Paris office. In the second sentence, there is only one company office and it is in Paris. (More about this in Chapter 9.)

PROBLEM ADJECTIVES:

Awful/awesome

Awful is an emotionally-packed word that offers a range of feelings from strange to terrifying to magnificent. It also is used as an intensifier, as in *awful happy. Awesome* is the word to use when you mean full of awe, inspiring, extraordinary.

Continual/continuous

Continual means without a break, while *continuous* means recurring periodically. Therefore, interruptions cannot be continual, they must be continuous. Gossiping on a production line could be continual, but must be limited in an office to continuous (or no work would get done).

Due to/because

Due is an adjective meaning adequate (due proof of loss), owed or owing (due on Friday), ascribable (due to a few people), directly (due north). It does not mean *because*. *Due* should be used only where an adjective modifier is needed.

The receipt was due proof of loss.
The payment, due on Friday, was three days early.
The riot was due to a few people with loud mouths.

Do not use *due to* when you mean *because* and want to show cause and effect.

Because the payment was early, it was credited early.
The shipment was late *because* of the strike.
Because of unforeseen circumstances, the strike was settled.

Eminent/imminent

People are eminent, that is, reputable, important. Events can be imminent, that is, about to happen, impending.

Famous/notorious

People can be either famous or notorious. If they are famous, we all know them, no matter how we feel about them. If they are notorious, on the other hand, they are disreputable, out of favor.

Fewer/less

Use *fewer* when you can count something.

He lost fewer pounds than his wife even though he ate fewer meals.
Use *less* when you can't count it or when the numbers are obscure.
She weighed less than he because she ate less at meals.

In 25 words or less is an idiomatic exception to this guideline. The term has been (mis)used in contest rules for such a long time, few notice it is grammatically incorrect. When such misuse occurs long enough, the term *idiom* is applied (to ease the minds of grammar teachers, no doubt).

Good/bad vs. well

Good is a hunky dory adjective; *well* is feeling good (a hunky dory adverb). The other *well* is an adverb describing to what degree something is done. *Bad* is just bad, unless you use jargon. Then bad is good and good is bad. (Don't ask! See Chapter 5.)

Healthful/healthy

A person has a healthy outlook on life, which leads to a healthful state of mind. In general, people are healthy, inanimate objects are healthful.

Later/latter

This is a spelling problem. *Later*, of course, means at a time yet to come. *Latter*, pronounced to rhyme with batter, refers to the second of two mentioned subjects.

Later, in Chapter 17, we'll learn to spell *later* and *latter*, the latter having two t's.

Liable/likely/apt

Shades of meaning separate these words. You can remember which is which by looking at the degrees of impact each has.

If a friend is apt to call you at midnight, there is a strong tendency for the behavior.

If a friend is likely to call at midnight, count on it; the probability is there.

If a friend is liable to call at midnight, be prepared for bad news. Liable has strong legal connotations and must be used carefully.

Lots

Grammar teachers for years have been trying to drown *lots*. Unless you deal in real estate (lots for sale), check your writing to avoid this. Verbal usage gets lost too quickly to check, but the overuse of the word indicates a lack of better adjectives, like *very*, *much*, *many*, *several*.

Most and almost

Most has to do with numbers; almost has to do with proximity.

Most of the crowd was *almost* on top of the stage.

Nice

If you have a good, standard, across-the-board definition for this, most people would like to know. *Nice* means something different for each person using it and each person hearing it. So play nice and find a more specific word.

It was a nice day. (Do you mean sunny, without problems, argument-free, productive, warm, cool, pleasant, challenging, or all of the above?)

Real

When using this word, ask yourself if you mean *not fake*. *Real* means that you aren't trying to put something over. It does not mean *very*. Most of the time we try to make it mean *very*.

This is a real opportunity to perform good works. (Not *real good* opportunity.)

Terrible

Like *awful*, this word means something nearly opposite the way it is used.

The food had a *terrible* taste. Full of terror? Come on!

If the food is *bad*, *sour*, *ishy*, say so, but stay away from *terrible* unless you mean evoking terror.

Their/your

Another spelling problem. The adjective pronouns *their* and *your* are possessives and are spelled without an apostrophe.

Take their advice and button your lip.

If you insert the apostrophe, you're (you are) making a contraction that they're (they are) not going to understand.

Viable

This very specific word has a very specific meaning—able to support life, capable of surviving, existing, developing. It comes from the words *vital* and *vivid*, meaning *to have life*, and it is used most often by biologists. Use *viable* in the context of living matter, survivability. In other contexts, use *plausible*, *possible*, *feasible*.

EXERCISES:
(Answers to exercises are in the Appendix.)

Jazz up these sentences with appropriate adjectives:

1. All the candidates were qualified.
2. Two of them—Kenneth Pease and Barbara K. Warren—stood out.
3. The Board members were in agreement.

4. The staff wondered about the decision.
5. President Valdez encouraged the Board to choose one candidate.

Choose from the following adjectives:

6. The Board had (lesser/fewer) reservations than ever before.
7. (These/This) new kind of candidate is impressive.
8. (These/This) new, young candidates showed talent and responsibility.
9. The (more/most) apt the candidates, the (fewer/less) difficult choices have to be made.
10. "Which candidate do you believe would go (farthest/furthest) in a career with Syntax?" they asked.

Insert hyphens to form appropriate compound adjectives:

11. Two final candidates could cause a head on collision among the already perplexed Board members.
12. Several do it yourself suggestions were made as tie breakers.
13. No one considered a do or die quick decision.
14. Let's just take one more raised hand vote.
15. The Board decided to hire both top notch candidates in one rash go to hell unanimous vote.

5

How Fast, Which Way?

ADVERBS

Adverbs are the easily identified forms of words that end in *ly*. But not all of them. Adverbs modify verbs, and they also can modify adjectives and other adverbs. In this chapter you'll find how adjectives and adverbs differ (bad, badly; good, well) and how they compare (fast, faster, fastest). There are some problem adverbs as well: *scarcely*, *hardly* and *barely*, *sure*, *smooth*, *very* and the ever-popular *really*. We will attack the use and overuse of *hopefully* in today's language. And we'll address adverb clauses and phrases.

The adverb enhances a verb, telling when something happened, where it happened, how or why it happened, to what extent it happened. When you see the *ly*, immediately look first for a verb. Adverbs modify verbs. What else!

There is something else. Adverbs also can modify adjectives and other adverbs. Adverbs are the words that tell why, when, how much, how far, how high, and so on. Therefore, it shouldn't be strange to expect them to tell how pretty, how expensive, how detrimental. And they do.

Adverbs are notoriously recognizable as adjectives with an *ly* ending (*notoriously*, an adverb that modifies the adjective *recognizable* which describes the subject *adverbs*). Adjectives describe: beautiful, thick, quiet, horrible, fantastic, loud. They become adverbs by adding an *ly*: beautifully, thickly, quietly, horribly, fantastically, loudly.

The beautiful child danced *beautifully*.
The mother *quietly* carried the quiet child out of the room.
The *horribly* disfigured monster produced an *unearthly* yell.

ACCURATE ADVERBS

She bored me *terrifically*.
That adverb is derived from the verb to terrify. Is that what is meant?
I found that the sales clerk was *awfully* nice.
Come on now, awfully? And didn't we dump *nice* back in Chapter 4?
He's a handsome man. If he looked (different/differently), I would be
    jealous.

Use *differently* if you mean the way he uses his eyes, and *different* if you
want him to change his appearance. *Different* (adjective) would modify the
pronoun *he*; *differently* would modify the verb *looked*.

COMPARATIVE ADVERBS

Comparative adverbs are formed in much the same way that comparative
adjectives are, utilizing endings of *er* and *est*. In the same manner, some
adverbs take kindly to booster modifiers, such as *more*, *most*, *less*, *least*.
How fast does the train go? Fast, faster, fastest.
How quietly did the children move? Quietly, more quietly, most quietly
or quietest.
Adverbs can be compared just like adjectives. One train travels faster
than another, but travels the fastest of three or more. Some children moved
more quietly than others, and a few moved the most quietly they had ever
moved.

The shopkeeper stared coldly at the intruder.
The shopkeeper stared more coldly at the intruder than at his clerk.
The shopkeeper stared the coldest at the intruder than he stared at any of
    the guests in the room.

Look at the difference between the following two sentences:

The doctor appeared (to be) calmer than the patient.
The doctor appeared more calmly than the patient (appeared).

In the first sentence, it is necessary to differentiate between using
calmer as an adjective modifying *doctor* or as an adverb modifying
appeared. That is achieved by the addition of *to be*. In the second sen-

tence, one would believe that the doctor appeared (poof!) slowly, calmly, while the patient boomed into the room.

If we use: The doctor appeared to be more calm than the patient, the clause *to be more calm than the patient* becomes the adjective modifier for *doctor*.

ADVERBS WITHOUT *LY*

A few adverbs exist without the benefit of the *ly* identity tag. For the most part they are short and easily recognizable. Occasionally, a grownup will recognize them as adverbs and try to tag them by using the *ly*. That's where we get the strange combinations that sound ostentatious and affected.

The words include: late, very, well, not, there, fast, quick, slow, close, deep, direct, fair, fine, hard, high, low, right, wrong, straight, tight, loud.

The following are grammatically acceptable, with clear meaning:

The sign warned to go slow. The officer warned to move slow.
The ball was hit deep into left field. He jammed his hands deep into his pockets.
If you want to catch the ball, move right (to your right, dunderhead!).
The sixth grade team did fine.

Of course many of these words have other meanings that will require the ly if used in the adverb form.

We moved slowly through the traffic.
The team felt deeply about the loss.
If you want to catch the ball, move rightly (smoothly, quickly, in the correct way).
The sixth graders performed like a finely tuned band. (Way to go, sixth graders!)

Warning: That little three-letter word *low*, which can be either adjective or adverb, turns around all the rules. Talk about a low pitched ball, mention how low the radio played, but add an *ly* and you don't have an adverb anymore. You have an adjective!

The lowly frosh wore a beanie and scored low (not lowly) on the SAT. Go figure!

ADVERB PHRASES AND CLAUSES

Just like the adjectives, adverb modifiers also come in phrases and clauses. (Remember the phrase usually begins with a preposition; the clause includes a verb.)

Johnson ordered breakfast *before nine.*
Johnson ordered breakfast *before he got out of bed.*
Johnson ate *with his fingers*, and scattered crumbs *in a very disorderly way* around the bed.

The italicized phrases and clauses modify the verbs that precede them. Which brings us to misplaced modifiers.

MISPLACED MODIFIERS

Sometimes a misplaced modifier is just plain funny. Sometimes it can be a disaster. The general rule is to place modifiers as close as possible to the words they modify. In the case of adverbs, they should be relatively close to the verbs they modify.

Johnson ate and scattered crumbs *with his fingers* in a very disorderly way.

The meaning has been shifted by moving the phrase *with his fingers* away from the verb *ate* and closer to the verb *scattered*.

The CEO agreed to meet with the dissident employees hesitatingly before lunch. (Confusing)
The CEO agreed hesitatingly before lunch to meet with the dissident employees. (Better)

TROUBLESOME ADVERBS

Hardly, scarcely, barely

These words are negatives and need to be treated like any other negative when complying with the rule about double negatives. Don't use double negatives. Therefore, if you use one negative word, you cannot use another.

She *scarcely* breathed as the dog showed its fangs. (OK)
She *scarcely didn't* breath as the dog showed its fangs. (Not OK)
He *hardly* had time to catch his breath. (OK)
He *didn't hardly* have time to catch his breath. (Not OK)

Hopefully

If you counted all the times that this word was misused, no one would ever get any work done. Hundreds of times each second, someone uses the word *hopefully* in the ungrammatical way.

This problem must be solved, hopefully soon.
Hopefully, this will not continue.

Hopefully is an adverb. The adjective is *hopeful*. The chances of the difference being observed in our daily language is not very hopeful. Just look for the verb that *hopefully* is asked to modify. Does it do its job?

The golfer stroked the ball hopefully into the hole. (OK, good shot.)
The golfer hopefully stroked the ball into the hole. (Question: Are we hoping the golfer stroked the ball, or was she hoping she would sink it?)

Really

A favorite adverb of English-speaking people is *really*. Another is *pretty*, as in *pretty far*, *pretty tall*. Watch out for those. Look closely at what you're saying and you'll probably discover that you really mean to use *very* or something more specific. The word *real* means actual, alive, not fantasy. We tend to use many adverbs carelessly. Becoming aware of what good adverb usage can do to your communication may be incentive enough to be more careful.

Real good

When something is referred to as tasting real good, it ought to taste delicious. Common usage passes *real good* as an idiom. "Everybody says it." Now you know that everybody can be grammatically wrong and remain in step with everybody else. Miss Miller might suggest that when something has been done right, use the adverb *well* and modify it with the more appropriate *very*. *That job was done very well* is preferable to *You done real good.*

Run smooth

Miss Miller warned us about using the adjective *smooth* to refer to the sound of an engine. Smooth usually means without wrinkles. Most dictionaries now include a definition that gives *smooth* a meaning of functioning without hindrance, including engines. However, be sure to use the adverb smoothly.

> The program closed smoothly.
> The transition of government was made smoothly.

While Miss Miller was cautioning about using the verb *run* with *smooth*, she hesitated to tell us why. Or maybe we didn't understand. As adults, perhaps we can follow the logic involved. *Smooth* is an adjective. (The adverb is smoothly.) Adjectives cannot modify verbs. Remember? Therefore, we should not say an engine runs smooth.

Likewise, we should not say that the car ran smoother than before. We need to use the adverb *smoothly* with the comparison word *more*. Which gives us:

> The car ran more smoothly than before.

Short, shortly

You can see where a dilemma might occur with words like these. *Short* has different dictionary definitions as well as different grammatical functions. It is one of the words that is an adverb with or without the *ly*. ·

> The board fell two feet short of the opening.
> The carpenter recognized shortly the need for new lumber.
> The carpenter spoke shortly to the lumberyard owner.

In the first sentence, *short* is an adverb indicating where the board fell. In the second, the adverb *shortly* modifies the verb *recognized*. In the third, *shortly* is an adverb meaning curt, rudely brief.

Surely

Surely is another troublesome adverb. Its root word is *sure*, defined as certain, secure, steady, inevitable, destined. Because it is related so closely to *certain*, we often equate it with *yes*. The word *sure* or *surely* can best be used when the meaning is closer to inevitability than to a simple *yes*. It's also a dandy word to use to indicate steadfastness and reliability.

Very

Very is a perfectly good adverb that is over-used when a more specific word would better tell the story, and under-used when it needs to show a greater extent. Some grammarians suggest that *very* should not be used to modify a word that has a verb root: displease, dislike, interest, grow.

Avoid: very displeased, very satisfied, very interested, very grown.

If you insist on using *very*, add another acceptable adverb (much or well) to modify a verb form. Restrict *very* or *well* to use with adjectives or another acceptable adverb: very much displeased, very well satisfied, very much interested, very well grown.

Her supervisor was *very much displeased* with the production report. (Much better than using *real*.)

The production record was *very nearly* twice what it was a year ago. (Much better than using *pretty*.)

Well/badly

The adverbs are *well* and *badly*. (Good and bad are the adjectives.) When something is done acceptably, it has been done well. If that something was not acceptable, the job was done badly. Both of these words modify verbs, describing how something was done.

Warning: When one enjoys good health, one feels well. This *well* has a completely different meaning. When one comes down with a bug, one feels bad, or sick, or miserable, or some other adjective! When referring to health, *well* is also an adjective. So is *bad*. (If you feel badly, your fingertips may be numb.)

Notice the different, sometimes twisted, meanings that occur when using the wrong form of the word.

The fish smells bad. (Find the air spray!)

The fish smells badly. (Poor fishy has a cold.)

The road appeared dangerous. (The road may be dark or full of ruts.)

The road appeared dangerously, causing us to swerve. (It made an unexpected appearance, suddenly, causing us to swerve.)

The chicken tastes crisp. (Ummm, good!)

The chicken tastes crisply. (It's little tongue shot right out there!)

TRICKY ADVERBS—ARE THEY OR AREN'T THEY?

Already is an adverb meaning previously. *All ready* means that everyone is prepared.

Formerly is an adverb meaning once upon a time. *Formerly* is an adverb meaning to behave in a formal manner.

Maybe is an adverb meaning perhaps. *May be* is a verb phrase suggesting a possibility of being.

Seldom ever doesn't make sense; the words are opposites. *Seldom* means occasionally; *ever* is a long time. What may be meant is *seldom if ever*, meaning there's a long, long wait ahead.

Too is an adverb that means excessive, extreme. Grammarians call it an intensifier. Too often, it becomes confused with the preposition *to* or the adjective number *two*. *Too* also means also.

Sincerely yours. While we're talking about adverbs, let's take a look at the ones that generally close business letters. They could be called Terms of Endearment: sincerely, cordially, truly, warmly, respectfully, ad nauseam. The good news is that they can be omitted, wiped out, left out, deleted, removed, dropped, forgotten. (For more about Terms of Endearment, see Chapter 19.)

EXERCISES
(Answers to exercises are in the Appendix.)

Select a more specific adverb to replace the indicated nerd-adverb to give the word (verb or adjective) it modifies a more accurate description.

1. Kenneth Pease was seeking a (really) high quality advertising agency.
2. He (surely) knew he wanted high standards.
3. In reality, he preferred a (very) prestigious agency.
4. He (really) directed his efforts toward Syntax.
5. Would he wind up (awfully) bored at a smaller agency?

Choose the correct adjective or adverb to make sense of the following:

6. Barbara Warren seemed (like/likely) to choose a larger agency.
7. She appeared (reckless/recklessly) in her choice of Syntax.
8. In the end, she believed (wholehearted/wholeheartedly) in her decision.

9. She thought she could (hardly/not hardly) consider a strong manufacturing clientele.
10. When she decided, she closed her eyes and pointed, (not scarcely/scarcely) breathing.
11. If she chose (wrong/wrongly) her career might be over.
12. Her career counselor spoke (direct/directly) to her saleable skills.
13. She wanted to go (straight/straightly) to New York.
14. Finally, she aimed (high/highly) and chose Syntax in Chicago.
15. When the call came, she realized how (close/closely) she had come to making the wrong decision.

Move the adverb, phrase or clause closer to the verb it modifies:

16. The president of Syntax agreed to hire both candidates in an enthusiastic way.
17. The candidates accepted the dual offer of the Board graciously.
18. The time was set for a day to begin work suitable to all of them by Valdez.
19. He spread the news to Elizabeth and Tony before announcing to the company secretly.
20. Hopefully the company looked forward to meeting their new associates soon.

6

The Little Words

PREPOSITIONS

It would be easy to include all the little words of three letters or less in this chapter, but it wouldn't quite be accurate. However, many of the prepositions *are* little words that make a big difference. These are the often-used words that point in a direction (up, down, to, from, on, at, in, out, over, under, between, among, above, below, etc.), and they are the words that introduce phrases. Some of the problem prepositions are *among* and *between, in* and *into, like, as* and *per* (ugh!). Problems too are the prepositions that follow verbs or adjectives to convey a specific meaning. Subtle but important meanings shift when such prepositions are used. This is where you'll find a new respect for the little word *up* (that can be deceptive in its meaning!) and another little word *down* that can assume the form of just about every part of speech.

Prepositions have one purpose in life: to show relation of an object to another word in a sentence. All of this leads to the belief that prepositions and their phrases are modifiers: some adjectives, some adverbs. These phrases function the same way as plain adjectives or adverbs.

Miss Miller taught you to remove prepositional phrases from a sentence while you're looking for the subject and verb. That's good advice. When determining how to handle verbs and subjects (singular, plural), ignore the phrases.

The minutes of the report, with several notations of a particularly inflammatory nature, (contain, contains) allegations that are untrue.

Remove the prepositional phrases to uncover the real subject, and the verb tense is easier to determine. The basic skeletal sentence, leaving out the prepositional phrases: *The minutes . . . contain allegations. . . .*

Isn't that easy?

Prepositions shouldn't give you trouble if you remember they are descriptive, require a noun or pronoun object (from Column B), and when used as modifiers need to be next to the term modified.

The trick of good writing is to control the use of prepositional phrases. Much writing is cluttered up with an overdose of them, many of which could be eliminated or turned into straight modifiers. The rule of thumb is to avoid using more than two or three prepositional phrases in a row.

She looked for a bank[1] with many offices[2] in the downtown area[3] of the city[4] near her company[5].

Five in a row are too many phrases. Re-write this sentence to incorporate a few phrases as single word modifiers:

She looked for a downtown multi-branch bank near her company.

As with simple modifiers, beware placing the phrases in an inappropriate spot. The above sentence could have been re-written to read:

She looked for a downtown bank near her company with many offices.

Because of its location, the phrase *with many offices* appears to modify *her company* when it actually modifies *bank*.

Modifiers need to be close to the words they modify.

Note too that we eliminated the phrase *of the city* since it seems to contain facts that are already evident.

DOUBLE PREPOSITIONS

Sometimes two or more prepositions are used for specific meanings: *according to* the weather report; *apart from* your plans; *instead of* an umbrella; *because of* the rain.

Be careful of using unnecessary, extra prepositions. Because they are small, we think we can use them just any old place; we tend to overuse them.

The rocks rolled off (of) the cliff.
Where have the boulders gone (to)?
She tried to tell me where it is (at). (See Ending With a Preposition)

TROUBLE PREPOSITIONS

All, any, or both

A common usage that may be difficult to purge is the extra preposition we use after the words *all* and *both*. Usually, if a noun follows, the preposition can be eliminated. If a pronoun follows, use the preposition.

> Ask all (of) the skiers to gather now.
> Ask all of them to gather now.
> When both (of) the ski jumpers meet, they smile.
> When both of them meet, they smile.

Among/between

Between requires a minimum and maximum of two people.

> Between us, Maizy is the most outspoken. (There are only two of us, Maizy and me.)

Among requires a minimum of three, with no maximum.

> The secret is safe among these listeners. (We aren't sure just how many, but we know it's three or more.)

Let's keep this between you and me (or is it between you and I?). Objects of prepositions take pronouns from Column B, which should settle the problem of which pronouns to use with prepositions. *Between* and *among* always take pronouns from Column B (the object).

> The decision is between him and her.
> We'll divide the responsibility between them and me.
> Try to keep this among you, her, Harrison, and me.

Courtesy requires me to put the first person pronoun at the end.

In/into

Confusion develops between the two prepositions *in* and *into*. *Into* implies movement, as moving *into* a situation or place. *In* indicates a position inside.

> We walked *into* the room; we then were *in* a strange place.
> While we are *in* this state of consciousness, we cannot go *into* a trance.

Like/as

An easy way to remember which word to use is to visualize. Use your mind to imagine what something is like. If you get a picture, use *like*. If you get a feeling, use *as*.

Here's the hint: as a preposition, *like* is followed by a noun or pronoun, (not by a clause). *As* is followed by a clause.

He behaved perfectly, like a model child. (noun follows *like*)
He behaved perfectly, as we knew he would. (clause follows *as*)
They dance like other people.
They dance as other people walk.
He had a deep voice like The Hulk, and as The Hulk, he turned in a
    great performance.
The pendant was shaped like a heart.
The pendant was expensive as we had expected.

Like is a dangerous word which needs careful handling. It will get more attention when we talk about word functions. (See Chapter 14.) This little four-letter word can take the role of seven of the eight parts of speech. No wonder it gives us trouble.

Per (ugh!)

Per is a preposition that means *through* or *by means of*. It has lost its original Latin usage, except in connection with numbers.

Use three board feet per unit.
The cost is $500 per hour.
Racing cars move up to 300 miles per hour.

Perhaps that is why some business people throw in a *per* every chance they get. It sounds official. In fact, it sounds quite pompous to say, "As per my instructions." or "That's allowable, as per the minutes of the board meeting."

Don't! Don't give in to the temptation to sound imperious. Use a more congenial *according to* or *as found in* instead.

According to my instructions.
That's allowable, as found in the minutes of the board meeting.

Per annum is acceptable only when used in connection with legal annual business. *The quota was set at $4 million per annum.* The same applies to *per diem, per capita, per mill, per se.* Each has its own meaning in the technical language of business.

Up

A favorite word of grammar teachers is the word *up.* Miss Miller used to say that it gives newcomers to the language more trouble than some of the big words. *Up* means to go the opposite of down, to rise, to incline, to move in a vertical way towards the sky. How then can you explain its use in the following:

> Please write up your reports at once.
> Don't give up on the secretary.
> She'll be tied up until long after closing.

Look at the differences and similarities between the following pairs: *shut up* and *shut down; burn up* and *burn down, get up* and *get down, up the street* and *down the street, slow up* and *slow down.*

Many verbs acquire an *up* tagged onto their backsides: ante up, clean up, close up, do up, drink up, hurry up, join up, keep up, line up, live up, lock up, mix up, offer up, pay up, play up, ring up, set up, stop up, sum up, tie up, tidy up, tilt up, turn up, wake up, wash up, work up, wrap up, up to now, up to us, and even *listen up.*

When some of these words are pushed together, they become nouns with their own meanings: cleanup, closeup, lineup, lockup, makeup, mixup, tie-up, wakeup, workup, wrapup.

When John makes up a story to explain the makeup on his collar, he'll make up with his wife while she makes up the bed and makes up her face after crying.

When the words are reversed, some of the combos retain their meanings; many don't. Consider: up ante, upbeat, upbring, upbuild, upgrade, upgrowth, upheave, uphold, uplift, upkeep, upmarket, up play, upraise, uprise, uproot, upscale, upshift, upspring, upstage, upstart, upthrow, upthrust, uptilt, upturn.

Computer language is setting a trend that places the preposition in front of the verb to make a new verb. Now we can download, offload, input, outbound, offclear, update, upscale and downscale. To a grammar-conscious listener, some of the language sounds weird. But to a computer operator, it's perfectly understandable.

Simple reversal of the words doesn't seem to retain similar definitions.

There is no connection between the meanings of *sweep up* and *upsweep*. One requires a broom; the other requires a comb, or an upward motion. *Set up* means to build; *upset* means the opposite.

Down

Down enjoys the same overuse as *up*, with the additional ability to pose as a number of other parts of language—noun, verb, adjective, adverb and preposition. One can *download, downplay, downgrade, downshift, downsize, downswing* and *downturn* (verbs). Nouns include a *downer, downbeat, down-bow, downdraft, downfall, downgrade, downhill, downside, downstage, downstairs, downtime, downtown, downtrend*, and a *downturn*. *Down under*, once considered an adverb which pin-pointed the location of Australia and New Zealand, has become a proper place noun, identified with capital letters: *Down Under*.

As a preposition, *down* is often used with other prepositions: *along, around, through, toward, in, into* or *on*:

down along the river   down around the bend
down through the ages   down toward the bottom
down in the pond   down into the depths of the pond
down on your knees   down among the sheltering palms

ENDING WITH A PREPOSITION

Miss Miller also warned against ending a sentence with a preposition. She needn't have bothered; it only confuses many of us.

Here's a Policy Statement:

Whereas many prepositions also are used with verbs as part of the verb; *And whereas* these verbs sometimes appear at the end of a sentence; *Therefore*, let it be here recorded that it is okay to end a sentence with a preposition, if it's not overdone.

She's the kind of person you can depend on.
He wanted a plan he could agree with.

These sentences would be awkward, stiff, if we tried to hide the preposition:

She's the kind of person on whom you can depend.
He wanted a plan with which he could agree.

Grammatically, these are great written sentences, but that's not the way we talk. The inclination is to write more like we talk: comfortably.

We risk straining something by trying to hide the ending preposition:

We didn't understand what he was asking about.
We didn't understand about what he was asking.

Or, as Winston Churchill is credited with saying, "That is something up with which I shall not put."

And the bane of Miss Miller's life in the '90s: *You just don't know where it's at.*

Use of this last example has taken off like a space ship and probably won't come down soon. The word *at* seems to be used as an intensifier. Instead of emphasizing the verb, the little preposition seems to add punch. *You just don't know where it is* emphasizes the verb. *You just don't know where it's at*, adds the punchy emphasis to the location.

Sorry, folks, we may have to live with this one. Call it an idiom, a colloquialism, modern usage, or slang. It'll be here for awhile.

IDIOMATIC EXPRESSIONS

When prepositions attach themselves to other words with no reason, they become *idioms*, the peculiarities of the language. There is no way to learn them other than to memorize them. Here are a few to ponder over (or is it *over which to ponder?*):

accepted by or at (not to)
accompany by (referring to people)
accompany with (referring to things)
acquaint with
acquit of (a charge)
adapted for (meaning suited to)
adapted from (meaning changed from)
adapted to (meaning adjusted to)
agree to (to consent or to accede)
agree with (harmony)
allude to
arrive at or in (not to)
at someone's house (not over, up, by)
cognizant of (not about)
coincide with (not on)

compare to (showing similarity)
compare with (examining two objects/people)
compensate for
comply with
consistent with
convenient for
convenient to (near)
conversant with
correspond to (be similar)
correspond with (write)
deal in (merchandise)
deal with (rather than about subjects)
depend on or upon
deprived of (not from)
destructive of (rather than to)
differ from (to be unlike)
differ with (disagree)
different from (although *than* is coming up strong)
discourage them from attacking (not to make an attack)
encroach on (or upon)
equivalent to (not with)
forbid you to do this (not from doing this)
graduated from (not graduated high school)
meanwhile or in the meantime (not in the meanwhile)
operate on or upon (when alluding to surgery)
identical with (rather than to)
in accordance with (not to)
indicative of
inferior to (not than)
in my opinion (not to)
in relation to (not with)
in respect to (rather than of)
in search of (rather than for)
insist on (or upon)
liable for (responsibility)
liable to (susceptible)
off (not off of)
parallel to (not with)
preferable to (not than)
related to (not with)
reminiscent of

responsible for
similar to (not with)
specialize in
talk to (to one speaker)
talk with
teaches at or in an institution (not teaches high school)

For more about idioms, see Chapter 14.

EXERCISES
(Answers to exercises are in the Appendix.)

Identify the prepositions in the following paragraph; determine whether the phrases introduced are adjective modifier (adj.), adverb modifier (adv.), verb addition (v.a.), infinitive verb (i.v.) or idioms:

1. Most of the people in the room had a healthy attitude about meeting the candidates who were about to arrive. Many whispered restlessly among themselves. Small groups huddled up to each other, sharing thoughts among themselves. Kenneth Pease arrived first, swaggering boldly into the crowd waiting at the door. He waved gallantly, smiled broadly and shook hands with the president of the company. When Barbara Warren, who pulled up in a stretch limo, rose to speak, she caused a hush to fall over the audience. Her appearance was stunning, like a breath of fresh air. Her hair was loosely tied in the back and her clothing resembled an Eastern princess. Did she dare think she would be able to convince anyone she was an executive?

Choose the correct word:

2. The group decided to walk (in/into) the president's office for the welcome.
3. The president waited (on/for) them in his office.
4. His plan was similar (to/with) one presented by his assistant Jeanette.
5. She certainly would be compensated (on/for) her advice.
6. Her plan differed (with/from) the president's only slightly.
7. She wanted (both/both of the) candidates to introduce themselves.
8. I could have fallen (off/off of) my chair.

9. The president's plan would be more convenient (with/to) the agency's time frame.
10. (All/All of the) office gossip was squelched as we listened.
11. How would this compare (to/with) what would happen tomorrow?

Rewrite this sentence to do away with the preposition jam at the end:

12. What did you bring that dilemma we didn't want to work out of up for?
13. Underline the word *down* wherever it appears in the following paragraph; then identify the part of speech being used (noun, verb, adjective, adverb, preposition):

Barbara, an avid football enthusiast, expounded during the Monday coffee break. The down-and-dirty opposition are expected to pull a downer before the game. They probably arrive down in the locker room wearing their down jackets and demanding successions of first downs. They ought to get down on their knees and hope the players down the ball before the third down or they won't get down the field to the touchdown line. They probably couldn't afford even the down payment on a football. If they were to shout, "Down with the tyrants!" you might assume they were down on the opposition, not forcing something down the throats of their own team.

7

Connectors and Expletives, Yeah!

CONJUNCTIONS AND INTERJECTIONS

How many conjunctions are there anyway? *And, or, but, nor.* Don't panic; there are others: *for, yet, so,* just for a start. Then there are the conjunctions that introduce clauses: *if, when, where, although, while, since, as.* And the conjunctions that introduce ideas: *therefore, nevertheless, however, otherwise, thus.* You'll hear about pairs of conjunctions and how they both must be used: *either/or, neither/nor, both/and, whether/or, not only/but also.*

What can be said about interjections, except *Yeah!* or *Ouch!* A point must be made to limit the use of interjections or risk losing effect. These are the words that can add emotion to writing, or make it look ridiculous, depending on how the interjections are used.

FIRST, THE CONJUNCTIONS

Conjunctions are the joining words, the connectors. A connector can join two words, two phrases or two clauses. The things being connected can be subjects or objects (nouns and pronouns), adjectives, adverbs, verbs or prepositions. What a connector produces is a compound: compound nouns, compound verbs, and so forth.

Compounds:

The painter and sculptor turns out to be the town mayor.

The compound subject noting there is just one person who is both a painter and sculptor requires a singular verb. If we said: *the painter and the sculptor*, we would indicate two people, we would still have a compound subject, but this would require a plural verb (since we're talking about more than one person).

The artist painted the hills *and* the trees. (compound object)

The watercolor *or* wash painting was sold at the auction. (The compound adjective indicates the single painting was either a watercolor or wash.)

The poetry was delivered lightly *but* seriously. (compound adverb)

Evelyn has sketched *and* painted all her life. (compound verb)

She has been in *and* out of galleries for two decades. (compound prepositions)

You could say she was in the limelight *and* out of money. (compound phrases)

She agreed to sell the painting, *for* she needed the money. (compound sentence—two independent clauses)

Notice in Chapter 15 how two simple sentences (independent clauses) can be joined in a number of ways to form a compound sentence. One way is with a comma and a conjunction.

The paintings were hung by the artist, *while* the gallery manager watched from the sideline.

If help were needed, she was there, *but* the artist was doing well by himself.

When adverbs are used as connectors, they also connect two simple sentences to produce a compound sentence. Such adverbs include: *however, consequently, therefore, nevertheless, while, since*, and more. Use them carefully to convey precisely the meaning you want.

Jerome studied at Julliard; nevertheless, he played badly.

Jerome studied at Julliard; therefore, he played badly.

Definitely different meanings are attained by using the wrong connector here. *Nevertheless* means *in spite of* (*however*); *therefore* means *in addition to* or *as a result* (*consequently*). *Furthermore, besides, moreover* mean *in addition to*; *otherwise* means *in other ways. While* means *during that time*, and *since* means *at a time in the past* or *from the time in the past*. Each connecting adverb carries its own shade of meaning.

Paired connectors

Some connectors must be used in pairs. That is, two connectors must be used to make it work: *either/or, neither/nor, both/and, whether/or, not only/but also*.

> The political point intended was *neither* to the left *nor* the right.
> *Not only* the Matisse *but also* the Degas were sold at the auction.
> *Both* Kafka *and* Proust are difficult to understand.
> We'll read them *whether* we understand them *or not*.
> We should *either read* them for content *or* we enjoy them for the scholarship.

In this last sentence the connector *either* is followed immediately by a verb. The sentence would read more clearly and observe the rules of parallelism if the second connector (*or*) also were followed by a verb.

> We should *either read* them for content *or enjoy* them for the scholarship.

> Aha! you are saying, now I know why that sounds better!
> Parallelism is a big topic in Chapter 15.

Adverb clauses

Some connectors connect dependent clauses to independent clauses. These connectors are joining things that are not equal. Remember how a *dependent clause* cannot stand by itself? It depends on the rest of the sentence to provide the subject. Some of the connectors used are: *if, when, where, whether, although, while, since, after, before, provided, because, unless, until*, and *as*. What they produce is a complex sentence. (More about this too in Chapter 15).

Such clauses are adverb clauses, modifying the verb of the main sentence. Like regular adverbs, these clauses answer questions of why, where, when, to what degree, for what purpose, with what result?

1. *If the party lasts longer*, we'll need more food. (The introductory clause modifies the verb *need* and answers the question *why*?)
2. *When the food arrives*, the party will last longer. (The introductory clause modifies the verb *will last* and answers the question *with what result?*)

Now let's turn the sentences around.

3. We'll need more food *if the party lasts longer.*
4. The party will last longer *when the food arrives.*

Each of these sentences contains a simple sentence and a dependent clause. In the first two, the dependent clauses appear up front and are called introductory clauses. (What else?) A comma follows the clause, dividing it from the main sentence. Notice that when the sentence is turned around (3 and 4), the clause falls behind the main sentence, and usually does not require a comma. When the clause appears in this way, it is recognized as nonrestrictive. That is, it could be left out and you would still have a complete sentence (although perhaps not the complete thought). Incidentally, that choice to use a comma or not depends on clarity. When you get to Chapter 9, you'll have a better idea of how to handle a choice like this.

Adjective clause conjunctions

Conjunctions also introduce adjective clauses. (And what do adjective clauses do, class? Modify nouns or pronouns, period.) Conjunctions used in adjective clauses are *who, which* and *that,* and they introduce clauses that come in two flavors: necessary and unnecessary.

A necessary clause contains information that is needed to identify the word it modifies. In other words, to leave out such a clause would cause problems in understanding.

The man *who was arrested* had mugged two people.
The victim *who lost his jewelry* filed the complaint.

Both of these clauses are necessary for identification.

An unnecessary clause containing information that is not needed to identify the modified word is usually set off with commas. To leave it out wouldn't harm the sentence; we would still understand.

Joe Underworld, *who was arrested*, had mugged two people.
John Citizen, *who lost his jewelry*, filed the complaint.

See the difference? In the last two sentences, we know that Joe had mugged two people and John filed the complaint. We could leave out the clause and not lose the sentence's message.

My argument was with the officer *who stopped my car.*
My argument was with the officer, *who stopped my car.*

In the first sentence, I'm arguing with the guy who flashed the blue lights. In the second, I'm arguing with an officer; while we were arguing he stopped my car.

The difference between *that* and *who* is apparent when we realize that *who* refers to a person and *that* refers to anything else.

The beautiful Leona, who Max adores, has arrived in her Jaguar.
The beautiful Leona, has arrived in her Jaguar, that Max adores.

What may not be apparent is the more subtle difference between *that* and *which*. Most of the time these pronouns are interchangeable.

The Porsche that is red belongs to me.
The Porsche which is red belongs to me.

However, consider the following:

The beautiful Leona, who drives a Jaguar, has arrived.
The beautiful Leona that drives a Jaguar has arrived.

In the first sentence, we are adding information about Leona; she drives a Jaguar. In the second sentence, the word *that* is a signal a clause that follows is essential and does not need commas. We are talking about a couple of Leonas and identifying the one that drives a Jaguar. When you want to identify someone or something in a group, substitute *that* for *which* or *who* and omit the commas. Such a clause stands out as an identifying clause and not a clause offering supplemental information.

The police car *that was in the accident* was a total wreck.
The police car, *that (or which) was in the accident*, was a total wreck.

In the first sentence we have to know that we are talking about the car that was in the accident, no other. In the second sentence, all we're interested in is that the police car was a wreck. The information that it was in an accident is supplemental.

Noun clauses

Conjunctions can lead off noun clauses too. Such a clause is always dependent since it may function as a subject or an object. It can also function as a description of a subject, that is, a subject complement. Conjunctions include *that, why, what, whatever, which, who, whoever.*

A noun clause is more like a multi-word subject. To untangle it, look for the verb and see who (or what) is doing it.

What she wanted depended on his generosity. (subject clause)

He gave her *whatever she wanted.* (object clause)

She is *whoever he wants her to be.* (subject complement. Both sides of the verb *is* are equal, reversible.)

Whatever she wanted was *what he gave her.* (double whammy clause, both the subject and the subject complement are noun clauses!)

So/so that (consequently)

So functions as both a connector and an adverb. When it is used as a connector (to join things), the meaning is *with the result that.* Many dictionaries propose limiting the use of *so* when it is meant to replace *so that.* Try it both ways. See which one you like better.

The guideline suggests using *so that* when introducing a clause that gives a reason for some action. However, many writers bemoan the overuse of the word *that.* In getting rid of this word, we seem to be irritating those who bemoan the use of *so* by itself. This may be one debate that remains open.

The painting is *so cluttered* nothing seems recognizable.

The painting is *so cluttered that* nothing seems recognizable.

Please clear up the painting *so* we can understand it.

Please clear up the painting *so that* we can understand it.

Yet

In Chapters 9, 10, and 15, the choice of a comma or a semi-colon between two simple sentences (compound sentence) will be discussed. Here, it is necessary to note that the choice of a semi-colon makes a more powerful statement of contrast. While this probably holds true for most connectors that join simple sentences, it is particularly true for *yet.*

Everyone disliked the exhibit, yet they contributed generously.

Everyone disliked the exhibit; yet they contributed generously.

Whether or not you use the comma or the semi-colon, the impact is worth considering as you decide.

And or but?

In their haste to get ideas down, writers sometimes give themselves away with an inappropriate choice between these two words. *And* joins things; *but* judges them.

> Your hair is pretty, *but* it hangs in your eyes.
> Your report was on time, *but* it is short.

But-clauses are readily identified as judgment statements. Psychologically speaking, whatever follows a *but* is a lie or a put-down. "This feels okay, but. . . ." "The food was fine, but. . . ."

Try reviewing your *buts* and changing them to *ands*. The impact often will be more positive and might even be helpful. It certainly will soften the put-down effect.

> Your hair is pretty, *and* it hangs in your eyes. (simple observation)
> Your report was on time, *and* it is short. (At least it doesn't sound like a put-down.)

Provided/providing

Both of these words can be connectors meaning *if*, or *as a condition*. While Miss Miller still preferred *provided*, either one is acceptable.

> The message was clear, *provided (or providing)* you understood the language.
> *Provided (or providing)* you met the requirements, you could join the club.

Unless

Don't mistake the preposition *except* for the connector *unless*.

> The bell will not ring *except* you wind the clock. (No!)
> The bell will not ring *unless* you wind the clock.

But what

This grammar problem, *but what*, is going the way of the crinoline petticoat. It is stiff and not appropriate in today's writing.

> I have no doubt *but what* the director could be right. (No!)
> I have no doubt *that* the director could be right.

Where or that?

The word *where* refers to location and should be used when referring to a place. Do not use it to substitute for *that*.

> They heard *where* the team had won the game. (No!)
> They heard *that* the team had won the game.

> You would be perfectly correct to use:

> They heard where the team was going. (location)

NOW FOR THE INTERJECTIONS: YEAH, EXPLETIVES!

Interjections are the surprise words. They contain emotional content that doesn't need an entire sentence to convey the intensity. Sometimes interjections are one word or phrase, sometimes a string of words. They are so important that a character on a once-popular children's show made up a song about "In-ter-jec-tions!"

Sometimes an interjection is so powerful it becomes an expletive (an interjection with a shady reputation). *Expletive deleted* became a part of the American language during the '70s Watergate hearings concerning the famous Nixon tapes. An expletive is usually the profane, extreme interjection. *Expletive deleted* is used parenthetically by the press to denote unprintable words.

The common, ordinary garden variety interjection (sometimes called an ejaculation in technical grammar lingo) can suggest surprise, annoyance, fright, wonder, confusion, pain. An interjection represents sudden and strong feelings.

> *Ouch!* That was no slap on the back!
> *Yahoo!* We won the account.
> The rush was sudden. *Gee whiz!*
> *Don't!* It's not ready to use.
> The customer fell, *splat*, right on the elevator floor.

Sometimes we consider introductory words as interjections. Examples include the one-word introductions of an idea or sentence: *really, for example, that is, yes, no, in fact, well.*

> *Really*, you shouldn't have tried so hard.
> *That is*, you should have expected a good response.
> *Yes*, I mean it.

It/there

While interjections are easy to identify when exclamation marks are used, there are a couple words that are considered interjections simply because of their meaningless use: *it* and *there*.

You became familiar with *it* being a neutral pronoun and *there* being an adverb telling *where*. However, a bad habit that has overtaken our language involves the overuse of these two words. Try to identify what you mean when you use these words, then replace them with more specific words to trim down your writing.

> *It* is a beautiful day.
> *There* isn't a cloud in the sky.
> We have *it* on good authority, the sun will stay out.
> Could *there* be a chance of rain?

When you use more specific words, not only does the meaning become clearer, but the rhythm of the words improves and gains depth. Listen!

> The day was full of sunshine. Not a cloud was visible in the deep blue sky. Authorities report the sun will stay out, without even a small chance of rain.

Specific words are usually better (see Chapter 14). In the case of replacing the interjections *it* and *there*, they are *always* better.

Like

When we wrestled with *like* as a preposition, we didn't realize it could also serve as an interjection. *Like* really! (Or is that a modifier to an interjection?) In recent years, the word has become a major part of our interjection repertoire.

> *Like, I'd never have thought of it that way, like I'm sure!*
> *Like, you didn't think I'd forget!*

EXERCISES
(Answers to exercises are found in the Appendix.)

Place the appropriate connectors in the spaces below. Watch the punctuation for clues.

1. Coming to work was more exciting, _____ the two new executives were arriving.
2. Kenneth _____ Barbara were to share an office.
3. "I don't like to be confined," said Ken, "_____ I will share the office."
4. In a tense situation, the newcomer moves slowly _____ the incumbents watch.
5. Anytime someone can smile _____ seethe, I'm impressed.
6. "Sharing is a challenge, _____ I enjoy trying," said Barbara.
7. _____ the generous Ken _____ the regal Barbara were smiling.
8. "Take me to the file room _____ I can review the agency performance," said Ken.
9. "That's _____ a wise _____ startling idea," retorted Barbara.
10. Work is a real challenge today, _____ too many people are crowding the newcomers.

INTERJECTION EXERCISES

Add an interjection to the following sentences to express an emotion or surprise.

11. "Your idea is definitely on the right track," said Elizabeth.
12. "Your remark was unnecessary," returned Barbara.
13. "You couldn't have thought of anything better," put in Ken as he tossed her a yellow pad.
14. "I dropped it," yelled Barbara.

Rewrite these sentences to replace the *it* and *there* when they are used as useless interjections:

15. "It feels a bit warm in here."
16. "There isn't a breeze of air conditioning in the room."
17. "I think I'll call it a day and go to my office," said Elizabeth.
18. "There is a pile of work waiting for me."
19. "It's just that it's the warmest season of the year," suggested Ken.
20. "If it were possible, I think there must be a way to rig up a fan," retorted Barbara.

8

Life's Little Headaches

VERBALS

Verbals backtrack to Chapter 3. However, they deserve their own chapter to fully cover the ways to construct them and the ways to use them. This chapter addresses the use of gerunds, participles and infinitives, the verbs that take on the behavior of nouns or adjectives, thus earning their label verbals. This subject, incidentally, has done in more than one inexperienced teacher.

Verbals are the cross-dressers of the grammar world. They are born as verbs, but take on the appearance and function of nouns and adjectives.

Verbals come in three flavors: infinitive, gerund and participle. (Sorry, we have to use such language!) Two of them, infinitive and gerund, are the *noun verbals*. The third, participle, is the *adjective verbal*. (Stay calm!)

The infinitive and gerund are perhaps the easiest. They both take verbs and, poof, turn them into nouns. They are easily recognized—infinitives by the *to* form and gerunds by the *ing* form.

THE INFINITIVE VERBAL

The infinitive form of a verb, to grammarians, is the way it is introduced, the basic form. It uses a *to* in front of the verb: to drive, to think, to be (or not to be). The infinitive verbal is the *to* verb behaving like a noun. That's it! "To be or not to be, that is the question." *To be* and *not to be* are infinitive verbs acting as nouns. Therefore, they are called infinitive verbals. (In the sentence that follows, *that is the question*, the word *that* is a pronoun replacing the nouns *to be* and *not to be*. The same applies to any *to* verbs that function as nouns, whether they are subjects of sentences, or objects.)

I've always wanted *to drive*. (object)
To think is to ask for a headache. (subject)

Split infinitives

One of the trouble spots with infinitives is the 7-10 split. It drives perfectionists mad. Most often, however, a split infinitive results in a slightly awkward sentence, even when it's used as a verbal. The advice most of the time is to avoid the split, but don't stay up nights worrying about it.

I've always wanted *to actually drive*.
Actually, I've always wanted *to drive*. (better)
I need *to deeply think* about my problems.
I need *to think deeply* about my problems. (better)

Complete infinitives

Another twist on the infinitive verbal is the use of the helping verb when the infinitive denotes something having happened prior to the real sentence verb: the complete infinitive. In the following sentences, the complete infinitive verbal is highlighted.

I want *to have driven before my next birthday*. (The real verb is *want*. The object noun phrase is *to have driven before my next birthday*.)
Harriet is believed *to have thought through her reply*. (The real verb is *is believed*. The object noun phrase is *to have thought through her reply*.)
Everyone is known *to have gossiped about the affair*.

THE *ING* VERBAL

The *ing* verbal—the gerund—is pretty much the same animal (no, gerbils are quite something else). Its identifier is *ing* at the end of a verb: driving, thinking, being. The dressed-up verb functions as a subject, object or complement, just like any well-trained noun.

At 16, *driving* was all I thought about. (subject)
Philosophers are devoted to their *thinking*. (object)
Everyone's favorite task is *writing*. (complement)

Careful now, don't get carried away. All *ing* words are not gerunds (nouns). Some *ing* words are straight verbs in the present ongoing sense.

You *are driving* me crazy. (verb)
I *am thinking* about you. (verb)
Everyone *is writing* their reports. (verb)

When using gerund phrases, not only is it necessary to put the gerund in the right place, but it is important to use the possessive case with nouns or pronouns you may choose to modify the gerund. Don't panic. Watch.

We knew about *Arthur losing* the election. (Losing is the gerund; Arthur modifies it; therefore, Arthur must be a possessive.)
We knew about *Arthur's losing* the election. (See, isn't that easy?)
We didn't know about *him leaving*. (Again, *leaving* is the gerund; the pronoun modifier must be a possessive.)
We didn't know about *his leaving*.
Delbert developing a job for him was a fine gesture. (No)
Delbert's developing a job for him was a fine gesture. (Okay. The subject isn't *Delbert*, but *Delbert's developing a job for him*.)

THE ADJECTIVE VERBAL

The past-complete verb (acting as an adjective) appears either as a single word with an *ing* or an *ed* ending or as part of a longer modifying phrase. (They were once called participles, but nobody has been able to figure out what that word means.) This verbal modifies nouns or pronouns only. That's why they are so easily identified.

The *rejected* suitor appeared crestfallen.
Everyone knew how the *wounded* fellow felt.
The *rejecting* lady had a reason for her actions.
That was why she gave the *whimpering* fellow his *walking* papers.

To be honest, they look just like regular adjectives and act like regular adjectives. What sets them apart is their verbal root word.

The complete-verb phrase behaving as an adjective is the one that causes problems, especially when it pops up in the wrong place. It must always be placed next to—as close as you can get—the noun or pronoun it modifies, or you are faced with a dangling participle (good gracious!).

The suitor *rejected by his friend* appeared crestfallen.
Everyone knew how the fellow *wounded by his love* felt.
(You see, when you add the phrase, the rest of the sentence can become

silly. This one needs to be completely re-written to get the verb away from the complete verb phrase.)

Everyone knew how he felt, that fellow *wounded by his love*. (Whew!)

Feeling rejected, the fellow returned to his partner to bury himself in work.

If we had said, *The fellow returned to his partner feeling rejected,* it would have appeared as if the partner were feeling rejected.

Having returned to work, he felt as if he could beat a buffalo.

How much better than: He felt as if he could beat a buffalo *having returned to work*.

There's a little twist to the complete verb. Whether you use the present tense or past tense makes a difference. When you use the present tense—having returned, having finished, having sensed—the word is a simple adjective modifier. When you use the past tense—having been returned, having been finished, having been sensed—the phrase is an adjective describing something that happened to the word being modified. *That word must be next to the phrase.*

Having been returned, *the package* was never identified. (Not: Having been returned, he never identified the package.) Ask what was returned? And you get the package, not he.

Having been finished, *the report* was laid on the president's desk. (Not: Having been finished, the president received the report on her desk.) What was finished? The report, not the president.

Having been overworked, *the typist* took off for the Bahamas. (Not: Having been overworked, the Bahamas seemed like a good idea to the typist.) Who was overworked? The typist.

ABSOLUTE PARTICIPIAL PHRASES

Now there's a word collection Miss Miller probably never used, at least in polite company. An absolute participial phrase is one that consists of a noun or pronoun with a participle (complete verb). It modifies the predicate of the sentence (that is, everything that isn't the subject, remember?) and it is awkward. Never mind the labeling; you probably recognize it.

Stay away from: *Sandy being the typist, the report was out on time.*

Instead use: *Because Sandy was the typist, the report was out on time.*

Sandy, the typist, got the report out on time.
No: *The moon being full, everyone acted like zanies.*
Yes: *Because the moon was full, everyone acted like zanies.*
The moon was cause for everyone to act like zanies.

PROBLEM VERBALS

Miss Miller used *dangling verbal.* Can anyone describe the thing? What is a dangling verbal anyway? And is it more serious than a misplaced verbal?

A problem verbal is the phrase (infinitive, gerund or participle) that appears too far away from the word or words it modifies (misplaced verbal), or does not relate to any words in the sentence (dangler). It is to be avoided.

When a sentence begins with a verbal phrase, the next word should be the word it modifies. The next word should answer the question who or what is doing the action.

When making cookies, you should mix the dough carefully.
While baking large quantities, turn the oven higher. (you is implied)
Having finished baking, you ought to clean the kitchen.
Yawning with fatigue, she turned off the lights.

Avoid:

When making cookies, the dough should be mixed carefully.
While baking large quantities, the oven should be turned higher.
Having finished baking, the kitchen should be cleaned.
Yawning with fatigue, the lights were turned off.

One of the reasons a written sentence needs to be read aloud is to avoid the kind of ridiculous-sounding sentence constructions that result from misplaced verbals. The following sentences seemed logical when they were written, but read them back and notice the confusion.

The patient responded to the doctor looking as if he were about to faint. (Who is about to faint?)
The child ran quickly to the teacher crying wildly. (Poor teacher! Or is it?)
While instructing the program, I am sure Terrence had the interest of students at heart. (I didn't actually instruct the program; Terrence did.)

Rubbing my hands to keep them warm, the carpool finally arrived. (Now really!)

Having broken his arm, the medics carried the boy to the ambulance. (Ouch! Rough medics.)

Having admitted me, the hospital took my vital signs. (Can a hospital do that?)

Okay, you get the idea. Read it back; read it aloud; put the modifier next to the modified!

EXERCISES
(Answers to exercises are in the Appendix.)

Underline the gerund or infinitive verbal (noun) in these sentences; label them G or I.

1. Building a reputation is important.
2. For years she wanted to enhance her own reputation.
3. Thinking it was easy aided in producing the visual image first.
4. Little did she know, looking good and being good are two different things.
5. Her goal was to start off the job with a bang.

Identify the infinitive verbals (nouns) in the following sentences.

6. To get along with Barbara has to be difficult.
7. If she wanted to make friends, they could work together.
8. She decided to choose the desk near the door.
9. When she wanted to move the furniture, he offered to help.
10. If she wanted him to help, she'd have asked.

Underline the participles (adjectives) in the following. Note whether they are single words (S) or phrases (P).

11. Determined to do this job, she accepted his help.
12. Outnumbered, he also had caught the fix-up fever.
13. Excited at the prospect, the two set to work the next Saturday morning.
14. They had worked four hours before they stopped to rest, resolved to finish in one day.
15. They actually enjoyed the hard work, delighted with the joy of working together.

Rewrite the following sentences with the modifiers where they belong.

16. Applied by the executives, the office had a new coat of paint.
17. They had painted over some bare spots inspired with creativity.
18. Kicking over the paint can, the room looked messier by the minute.
19. Feeling tired, one side of the office didn't look as good as the other.
20. Having finished by late Saturday, the janitor saw the painters spatter paint on each other.

Part 2

PUNCTUATION

The most important part of road safety is the signing system. The same applies to the signing system of written communication. Without the little dots and dashes, readers become confused.

In speech, you can shrug your shoulders, whisper, sneer, smile, scowl, hesitate, scream, chatter, drawl or clip, adding emphasis or de-emphasis to what you're saying. In writing, all these nuances must be and can be done with punctuation and strategy. The more you read the work of good writers, the more you learn about the techniques. The more you practice the techniques, the more adept you will become at expressing yourself through written communication.

Some people are orators, speechmakers, swayers of vast audiences with their voices. They know and practice good punctuation, verbally. Only the great writers know how to practice good punctuation on paper to get a similar effect.

This section looks at the punctuation signing system, using familiar terms and examples. The catastrophe of a misplaced comma, for instance, is sometimes a surprise to writers who have been putting the little markers into their writing with abandon all these years. *Commas* are the punctuation road hogs, taking up the greater share of punctuation guidelines.

Colons are the headlights that point out what lies ahead. *Periods* are the complete stop at intersections; *semicolons* are the California stop that is longer than a comma, but shorter than a period. (A *California stop* is a half-hearted slow down at a stop sign.)

The voices of writing are the *question* and *exclamation marks.* They provide inflection to the written words that make the trip interesting.

Enclosures will be discussed: *quotation marks, parentheses and brackets.* You'll discover the different functions that each contributes to written communication.

In addition, we'll look at a variety of dots and dashes that offer their own special meanings to written language: *apostrophes, ellipses, hyphens, dashes and diagonals.*

Typesetting symbols and road signs are slightly different from typewritten or handwritten symbols. Some of these differences will be pointed out for users of computers (which mirror typesetting ways).

Don't underestimate the power of these tiny marks. More litigation than one would anticipate is brought into courts to contest their uses. Effective writers learn not only to read the road signs, but know how to use them to their best advantage.

Each chapter closes with a challenge to try punctuating some sentences by yourself to see how much easier you'll find it after you have reviewed the rules and developed your own guidelines.

9

The Reflective Pause

COMMAS, COMMAS, COMMAS

If one punctuation mark were more important than the others, it might be the comma, simply because it has more rules about it than any of the others. In this chapter, you'll find commas used in items in a series, to identify unnecessary phrases, before the conjunction to join two simple sentences, after an introductory adverb clause or verbal phrase, to separate items in an address or date, around parenthetical ideas, and wherever needed to clarify and prevent misinterpretation.

In a popularity contest for punctuation marks, the comma would win hands down (or tails down, as the case may be). The comma has more uses than any other mark of punctuation. It is the breathing space, the separator, the pause that explains. One grammar textbook considers the comma so important it devotes eight separate chapters to it.

Writers who cannot control the comma may be in danger of having their work misunderstood.

Some writers use too many, dropping them in like raisins in a scone, at random, whenever the mood strikes, and they don't care where they land.

Others like James Joyce never use commas or any other punctuation for that matter preferring to let the reader guess where the pauses should be.

Re-read the last two sentences, removing the commas from the first and placing them randomly in the second. Like this:

Some writers use too many dropping them in like raisins in a scone at random whenever the mood strikes and they don't care where they land.

Others, like James Joyce, never use commas, or any other punctuation, for that matter, preferring to let the reader guess, where the pauses should be.

The first sentence is quite readable without the commas. The second sentence makes the reader work to understand.

The use of a comma has held up national political conventions while planners hack out a party platform, making sure the commas are in the right places to serve the right purposes.

Imagine the difference between the two following sentences:

1. All members of the party who are eligible to vote will appear at the auditorium with their ballots.
2. All members of the party, who are eligible to vote, will appear at the auditorium with their ballots.

Guess how many people who understand commas will appear after reading the second sentence. The second sentence announces that all members of the party may vote. The first sentence limits the ballots only to those who are eligible. (Note: The first sentence of this paragraph mentions the people who understand commas, not the people, who understand commas, because all people don't understand them.)

Consider these:

If you want to tell Clarice, we cannot hold you back. (Clarice doesn't know yet.)

If you want to tell, Clarice, we cannot hold you back. (Clarice has the secret.)

No, I don't have any honey. (I'm out of honey.)

No, I don't have any, honey. (I'm out of whatever we were talking about, dear.)

No one should have to guess where the commas belong. That's why some rules are helpful. However, only the writer can determine the intended meaning of what is written, and that's why breaking the rules is often okay—to provide individual emphasis.

Since we now understand the problem, let's clarify this important little dot-with-a-tail that can confuse or amaze with its many uses. What follows is the framework of guidelines with which you can provide your own cosmetics, remembering that, like makeup, the less conspicuous the better.

COMMAS IN A SERIES

The comma is used to separate items in a series of three or more: one, two, three or more. While that seems clear enough, it raises the question of whether or not to use a comma before the final conjunction.

All the team—Tim, Tom, Todd, Terry and Trey—went to the game together. (Clearly there are five members on the team.)

Team members Tim, Tom, Todd, Terry and Trey walked off with all the trophies. (If we know there are four trophies, we know that Terry and Trey shared one. If we don't know that, we might assume there are five trophies.)

Team members Tim, Tom, Todd, Terry, and Trey walked off with all the trophies. (The extra comma after Terry explains that each one received a trophy.)

The question of commas is critical in legal documents. Imagine you are Rufus or Ralph mentioned in the following will.

The children will share my bequest of $4 million: Ruthanne, Rosy, Rufus and Ralph.

Do Rufus and Ralph each receive $1 million? Or do they split one-third of the bequest? Without the comma after Rufus, there is legal doubt about how the money is to be divided, into fourths or thirds. And that is how attorneys earn their fees.

You don't need that last comma before the final conjunction as long as the meaning remains clear without it.

The dinner special includes salad, chicken, rice and peas.

While this isn't earth-shaking information, there may be a time you would want to know if the rice and peas are a single dish or if they are separate. A comma after rice separates it from the peas if it is important to do so. If it makes a difference to know that rice and peas is a single dish, move it forward in the series, to read: The dinner special includes rice and peas, salad and chicken.

When the parts of a series contain commas of their own, you'll use a semicolon to separate the larger parts.

We're touring Austin, Texas; Little Rock, Arkansas; Wichita, Kansas; and Tulsa, Oklahoma.

Company officials are Jane Rockford, president; Rockford Howard, vice president; Howard Wichita, general manager; and Wichita Ryder, sales manager.

UNNECESSARY PHRASES/CLAUSES

Commas are used to separate unnecessary phrases from the words they modify, in much the same way as parentheses. Unnecessary phrases, sometimes called nonrestrictive, are those that could be omitted without damaging the sentence. While they contain additional information about the sentence, they aren't grammatically necessary.

1. Put the fish, Mix and Max, into the big tank.
2. The bucket, painted blue for male fish, is in the corner.
3. My husband, Wyman, will check the tanks tomorrow.
4. You could do that work, moving fish, after hours.

All of the above phrases between the commas are considered (grammatically) unnecessary and require the commas to say so.

Necessary (or restrictive) phrases, on the other hand, must be included in the sentence for clarity and are not set off with commas.

5. Put the fish Mix and Max into the tank. (In this case there may be several fish and we're asking only for these two. In the first sentence about Mix and Max (#1 above), these two were the only fish around.)
6. The bucket painted blue for male fish is in the corner. (This bucket, again, is one among many but is the only one painted blue.)
7. My husband Wyman will check the tanks tomorrow. (Oh-oh! In the sentence about Wyman [#3], the commas indicated that Wyman is the only husband we're talking about; there may be others. In this version, without commas, Wyman is my husband, my one and only husband.)
8. You could do that work moving fish after hours. (The example with the comma [#4] added an unnecessary adjective phrase to modify work and is therefore set off by commas to show it is not necessary to the sentence. To specify the work moving fish, the commas must be omitted.)

Notice the following sentence pairs.

The trouble that you caused cannot be overlooked. (Necessary clause)
The trouble, that you caused, cannot be overlooked. (Unnecessary clause)

In the first, without commas, the subject is *the trouble that you caused*. In the second sentence, the subject is *the trouble*. The unnecessary phrase set off by commas becomes the adjective modifier for *trouble*.

The argument is about Malcolm who loves chase scenes and me.
The argument is about Malcolm, who loves chase scenes, and me.

Malcolm in the first sentence appears to love both chase scenes and me. In the second sentence, the commas make clear that we are talking about an argument about Malcolm and me. Oh yes, he loves chase scenes.

The elephants which you fed on Tuesday came down with a tummy ache.
The elephants, which you fed on Tuesday, have been moved to another zoo.

In the first sentence, we are talking about the specific elephants which you fed on Tuesday. In the second sentence, the important information is that the elephants have been moved. The fact they were fed on Tuesday is unnecessary to convey the meaning.

This may help answer questions about whether or not to use commas to set off the clauses that follow. Using this simple guideline, can you tell which of the following Georges is courting trouble for having more than one wife?

George's wife Elsie was a good cook.
George's wife, Elsie, was a good cook.

You're right. The first George is monogamous. The second George is indicating with commas that he has at least one other wife. We don't know if the others can cook or not.

TO JOIN SIMPLE SENTENCES

Simple sentences, sometimes called *independent clauses,* can be joined to keep similar ideas together. To join two or more sentences, you have two choices: 1) connect them with a comma followed by a conjunction, or 2) connect them with a semicolon and no conjunction. The two sentences being joined should be so closely related that you want them to be together, not separated by a period.

Look at this punctuation in terms of driving a car. The punctuation signifies varying degrees of slow-down or stop for the reader. The comma with the conjunction is a slow-down, and the semicolon is a California stop; the period is a complete stop.

> The two cars collided at a busy intersection; three witnesses called it a fender-bender. (Two simple sentences connected with a semi-colon [California stop].)
> Two cars collided, and both front headlights were broken on one car, and the other car didn't appear scratched. (Three simple sentences connected with comma/and.)

The comma before the conjunction tells the reader that a new sentence is beginning. Sometimes the subject changes, sometimes a pronoun is used in place of the former subject. (Without a subject change, the sentence may be a simple sentence with two verbs, not requiring a comma: Two fenders were demolished on one car and had to be replaced.)

AFTER AN INTRODUCTORY ADVERB CLAUSE

Notice the word *introductory*. This guideline applies only to adverb clauses or single adverbs at the beginnings of sentences, not within or at the end of the sentence.

> Since everyone is here, we can begin the party.
> While you're eating, remember who did the cooking.
> After you're finished, clean up your dishes.

The following clauses, if placed at the ends of the same sentences, would not require commas:

> We can begin the party since everyone is here.
> Remember who did the cooking while you're eating.
> Clean up your dishes after you're finished.

AFTER AN INTRODUCTORY VERBAL CLAUSE

A verbal clause must be followed by a comma and the subject being modified. The introductory verbal clause may or may not lose its meaning if moved behind a sentence. What it loses, if moved, is the comma as well as the proximity to the subject being modified.

> Provided he leaves now, *he*'ll not be pursued.
> Determining to interrupt the conversation, *she* coughed until we noticed her.
> Disgusted with the display, *the others* left the party.
> Pacified, *she* returned to her corner. (Even a one-word phrase deserves a comma.)

Sometimes moving the clause behind the main sentence works:

> He'll not be pursued provided he leaves now.
> The others left the party disgusted with the display.
> She returned to her corner pacified.

Some clauses, if moved, can wreak havoc and are sometimes referred to as dangling.

> She coughed until we noticed her determining to interrupt the conversation.

OTHER INTRODUCTORY WORDS

One-word adverbs or adjectives also get a comma when they begin a sentence:

> Reluctantly, she gave up her seat at the piano.
> Slowly, she walked off the stage.
> Entranced, the audience was silent.

These same introductory words, if placed closer to the modified words, would require no commas but would have less impact.

> She gave up her place at the piano *reluctantly*.
> She walked *slowly* off the stage.
> The *entranced* audience was silent.

Interjections and expletives at the beginning (or end) of a sentence also are set off with commas:

Yes, she did have a raging virus.

Indeed, she could have stayed home.

Do you think the concert would have been the same, honestly?

She never would have told us, in fact.

Damn, we should have seen it coming.

SEPARATE ITEMS

Commas are used to separate items in addresses, dates, titles, measurements, and all manner of odds and ends.

Use a comma in addresses between the street, city and state: 987 Main Street, Bismarck, North Dakota. Or: Bismarck, ND. But, do not use a comma between the two-letter state abbreviation and the zip code in addresses: Bismarck, ND 58501. (The post office now is asking us to use all capital letters and no punctuation in addresses on envelopes.)

Use a comma to separate the date from the year only if both the month and day are used: July 24, 1950. Do not use a comma if only the month and year are used: July 1950. (Incidentally, with complete dates do not use a *th, st, rd*, or *nd* unless you omit the month. You'll pronounce it July 24th, but write it July 24. Use the *th* only if you omit the month and use the 24th—I'll see you on the 24*th*.)

Use a comma to separate names from titles: George Washington, President; Harry Truman, vice president; Henry Jackson, senator. Do not use commas if the title precedes the name: President George Washington, Vice President Harry Truman, Senator Henry Jackson.

Use commas in measurements to separate various components: 6-feet, 3-inches; 13 pounds, 7 ounces; 47 yeas, 47 nays, 6 abstentions.

PARENTHETICAL IDEAS

Ideas that come along in the midst of a sentence, like this, require commas to set it off. It only makes sense, we believe, to assume as much. If you object, however, you may want to eliminate the little nuisances. But you may, for sure, expect trouble.

Re-read those sentences without the commas and you get:

Ideas that come along in the midst of a sentence like this require commas to set it off. It only makes sense we believe to assume as much. If you object however you may want to eliminate the little nuisances. But you may for sure expect trouble.

TO CLARIFY AND PREVENT MISINTERPRETATION

Any time a sentence can be misread without a specified pause, you'll need to so specify with a comma. The choice is the writer's. The best way to catch such situations is to read the sentence aloud (or read it several hours after writing it).

> I'm sorry it's not loaded Rebecca.
> I want to be a hit man.
> Expecting company she didn't want to be undressed or caught with her hair uncombed.
> Delighted he brought flowers for the hostess who was not expecting such civilities.
> I'm not sure she never knew about that Valerie.
> While I froze my wife raised her purse and hit the assailant.
> Just as she was about to leave her husband walked in with opera tickets.
> They recognize the dilemma was a mutual misunderstanding and agree to keep their lives open from here on thanks to caring neighbors.

EXERCISES
(Answers to exercises are in the Appendix.)

Put some commas in the best places:

1. The next weeks apart from small squabbles passed uneventfully.
2. Barbara settled into doing what she does best selling.
3. Kenneth attempting to appear nonchalant bypassed Barbara at every chance.
4. Of course James Valdez believed he had made an impeccable choice.
5. "Yes Elizabeth Ken and Barb are working well together" he was heard to remark.
6. "If you listened surely you'd come to the same conclusion" he told her.
7. Every sale carried a triple bonus: a cash percentage gift certificates luggage and a vacation in the Caribbean.
8. Working at Syntax less than two months Barb had overtaken Ken and would you believe it shot out ahead.
9. While handling three clients at a time Ken contrived to work on the annual report due in six weeks.

10. Furthermore he redecorated their office using fourteen 1 x 6 shelves which carried books weighing up to 76 pounds 6 ounces.

11. By the end of six months Ken had moved into a new apartment at 123 Maple Street Chicago IL 99900.

12. On the other hand Barb was still rooming with an old college friend Skipper Hoover.

10

Headlights, California and Complete Stops

COLONS, SEMICOLONS, AND PERIODS

The colon is the road sign that says something follows. Generally, only two guidelines apply: to introduce a long direct quotation and to follow a formal introduction that includes words like *the following*. Be aware that the latter is one that invites controversy among the grammar pros.

Semicolons sometimes get mixed up with colons, but they have their own special uses. This is where we take on the troublesome compound sentence with its two separate and distinct parts. Some refinements here might surprise even a seasoned writer. Use the semicolon to separate items that contain commas within a list. And use the semicolon before an expression such as *for example, that is, for instance*. Semicolons are invaluable in separating a series of clauses that perform identical functions and are introduced with the same connective. In short, this combination of period and comma functions as an extra-powerful comma.

The use of periods is probably the simplest of the punctuations. Periods are used at the ends of sentences, after words that pass for sentences, as part of abbreviations, as decimal points, and in lists and outlining.

COLONS (:)

Can you think of colons as headlights? A colon has two little dots that indicate something is coming ahead; it acts like headlights on the road. Use a colon to indicate that an enumeration, a quotation (particularly, a long one), an example or an explanation will follow. Prepare your reader with words such as: *such as, as follows, the following, these things.*

You can select lunch from a wide variety of these gourmet items: pastas, salads, French and Italian entrees, and French dessert pastries.

People will request substitutions such as: red meat, peas and carrots, French fries, and coffee.

The article in the Tribune clearly stated the following: "The environment will be destroyed by plastic."

Do not use the colon, or any other punctuation, if your list directly follows the verb. The following sentences do not need punctuation:

The things that bother me *include* an empty coffee pot, difficult customers, and unappreciative bosses.

The most difficult people *are* unfriendly, surly, demanding, rushed, preoccupied and pompous.

Whether or not a capital letter is used after the colon depends on three factors: 1) If what follows is a quotation, use a capital letter: "That's what it's for."; 2) A complete sentence following a colon requires a capital letter; or 3) If you think that what follows is important enough to merit a capital, use it. The only grammar rule to follow is this: Know what you mean.

Sometimes, when what follows is only a word or two, you may consider using the long dash instead. Some punctuation authorities consider the dash to be more informal than the colon. Use your own judgment.

There was only one person responsible—the manager.

There was only one person responsible: the manager.

Quotations: Long and Short

In the matter of quotations, if the quotation is the standard use of dialog, a comma should follow the *he said* and *she said*.

Ray Bob marched through town saying, "Yea, yea, today's the day!"

Use the colon only if you are quoting some words in the midst of a narrative, as in a business report.

The chair opened the meeting with these words: "Let's do it."

You may quote whole passages or long dialogs using the colon, as long as it is preceded with the headlight words such as: *as follows, the newspaper account read, the speaker stated*, or similar words.

The meeting was opened with this admonition: "Only those delegates who are prepared to vote the entire agenda are welcome today. We have a long day ahead and we need everyone here. Please review the issues and be prepared to participate."

If a long quote is indented following the colon, quote marks can be omitted.

The speech was presented as follows:
Thank you for inviting me here this evening. I am so happy to be able to bring you this message on behalf of the many voters who will sweep me into office next November.
You realize, of course, that to gain this sweep, we need to begin working now to build up voter confidence.

The Colon to Separate Numbers

Use the colon to separate hours from minutes when referring to time:

12:15 P.M., 3:30 A.M., The mile was run in 3:58:07.

Use the colon to indicate ratios:

The vote passed 2:1.
Interest in the process was expressed in a 5:4 margin.

Use the colon when depicting chapter and verse:

The passage came from Psalms 3:5.

The Colon in Subtitles

Book and magazine titles often carry subtitles, which are set apart with a colon.

The Angry Angel: A Story of Retribution
Fragile Marble: An Environment Picture

THE COLON IN SALUTATIONS

The use of punctuation in salutations in business correspondence is changing from the more formal colon to the comma. When you wish to indicate a formal approach, use the colon.

Patrick Pedersen:
Dear Customer:

However much we may wish the terms of endearment to disappear (the dear in the salutation, the other endearments in the closings) many businesses continue to use them. Please don't confuse your letter recipient by using the endearing *Dear* followed by the formal Ms. or Mr. and then the also-formal colon.

Today's business letter writer often uses the recipient's name—the first name only if very friendly, or the complete name if more businesslike. By choosing the colon or the less formal comma, the writer further indicates the level of communication being used. Consider the difference between the following:

Janet Armstrong:
Thank you for the interview yesterday.
Janet Armstrong,
Thank you for the interview yesterday.

In Chapter 19, you'll find further discussion about ways to select the tone of a business letter and the impact you want.

SEMICOLONS—THE CALIFORNIA STOP (;)

The semicolon is the pause between the brief comma breath and the full period stop. It contains both marks and tells the reader to pause longer than a comma, but not as long as a period.

The prime purpose for the semicolon is to separate two complete, simple sentences (sometimes called independent clauses). There are times when two sentences will interact or depend on each other for specific meanings. When both sentences can stand by themselves, use the semicolon alone to connect them.

The garden blooms the year around; most seasons it is filled with roses.
The employee cafeteria is open daily; its food is the best around.

For contrast, the above examples could have been written in two other ways: as separate sentences, or as a compound sentence (with two simple sentences joined with a comma and a conjunction).

The garden blooms the year around. Most seasons it is filled with roses.
    (Two separate sentences.)
The employee cafeteria is open daily, and its food is the best around.
    (Compound sentence joined with a comma and conjunction *and*.)

The semicolon indicates a relationship between the two sentences and the need to keep them somewhat connected.

Transition Words and Semicolons

Transition words are what tie ideas together, show relationship, indicate shifts. These include such words as: however, therefore, yet, moreover, as a result, in addition, in summary, on the contrary, besides, consequently, for example, for instance, accordingly, also and many more.

When the second part of a compound sentence begins with a transition word or phrase, choose the semicolon. Because this pause is longer than a comma and shorter than a period, the reader can easily determine the connections between the clauses.

The meeting was long; nevertheless, the chair never slowed down.

Several people were commended; consequently, our interest never wavered.

No one was surprised; on the contrary, we all expected the long agenda.

Writers are more readily inclined to omit using the comma after one-syllable transition words. For example:

Sandwiches are seldom delivered later than noon; yet today the caterer was late.

The caterer was two hours late; thus we'll find another one tomorrow.

The food is excellent at this place; still we can't have it arriving late.

Before rushing in to use the semicolon, make sure that both sentences are able to stand by themselves and that the transition word(s) is not just a parenthetical expression. The following are not pairs of simple sentences.

Sandwiches are seldom delivered later than noon, however, until today.

The caterer, who was two hours late, furthermore, was willing to give us the food at half price.

The food is excellent at the other place, moreover, and cheaper.

Semicolons Prior To a Series

Here is a fine point that may be recognized by only three people in the world—Miss Miller, the author, and now you. The semicolon is also used prior to a series. It is used before certain expressions that announce a series coming up: *for example, for instance, that is* or *that is to say, namely,* and the Latin abbreviations, *i.e.* (that is), and *e.g.* (for example). Use a comma following these announcement words.

Use tall flowers in a large garden; for example, cosmos, dahlias, certain roses, and daisies.

I'd never consider bulbs; namely, daffodils, tulips or hyacinths.

Don't forget the herbs; i.e., lemon root, thyme, marjoram, and sage.

Certainly, this is fine-tuning punctuation. While Miss Miller probably didn't go into these finer points, somebody somewhere might have run them before you during the high school years. These fine-tuners indicate the difference between a good and an excellent user of grammar.

THE SEMICOLON IN A SERIES

The semicolon is used like a super-comma when the series already is filled with commas. Use the semicolon to avoid confusion with lists and series of times and dates, cities and states, names and titles.

Dates for interviews will be Tuesday, March 5; Wednesday, March 13; Monday, April 12; and Thursday, April 22.

They'll be held in Richmond, Virginia; Albany, New York; Columbus, Ohio; and Des Moines, Iowa.

We'll be replacing Zack Anderson, president; Anne Bacon, vice president; Bill Chandler, secretary; and Carol Dawson, treasurer.

The semicolon also works to organize a less-than-clear series of items.

We are looking for people who can work by themselves, without constant supervision; complete their work on time, as well as within the budget; attend evening meetings, which may be held at the office or in a restaurant; and who can write reports to be delivered to the Board of Directors.

Note that in this long, involved sentence, the subject and verb were repeated toward the end to remind the reader what the heck is being talked about. Sometimes in an eagerness to get everything in, we forget that the reader can easily become lost in lengthy complicated sentences.

PERIODS—THE COMPLETE STOP (.) AND OTHER DOTS

Question: How much trouble can a little dot cause?

Answer: As much as a complete stop in traffic. Like that traffic jam, you won't get in trouble with the period as long as it happens where it is supposed to. What's interesting about the period are the many instances where it should not be used.

The period is used after a general sentence, a statement, request or command.

One size fits all.
Everyone needs a new suit of clothes each year.
I'd like at least one new thing each season.
Don't try to tell me what to buy.

The period is also used after a fragment of a sentence that you want to resemble a complete sentence.

Certainly, each season.
Yes, definitely.

Abbreviations

The period also indicates an abbreviated word: etc., Mr., Ms., Sr., Jr., e.g., i.e., Inc., Ltd. Corp., Jan., Feb., Mar., Sun., Mon., Tues. The period is used in some letter abbreviations, sometimes: U.S.A., E.E.O.C., U.M.W. However, computerization is removing the periods from most abbreviations. It's best to check with the representative group when using the abbreviations.

Do not use periods in easily recognized capital-letter abbreviations: FAA, CPA, USA, NATO, YWCA, UFO, FDIC, IRS, FBI, nor in easily recognized small-letter abbreviations: rpm, mph, rbi, mpg.

The period is not used in postal abbreviations for states: WI, CO, KS, MN, OH, MD, FL, WA. You still may use them in regular abbreviations: Wis., Colo., Kans., Minn., Md., Fla., Wash.

New technology has provided us with at least one new abbreviation without a guideline to print it—facsimile transmission. FAX or fax—do we capitalize it or not? Do we abbreviate it with a period or not? FAX. or fax.? As long as it remains a word not registered as a trademark, spelled it with small letters—fax—preferably without a period.

Another note about abbreviations. Before you use one that may not be generally understood by your reader, be sure to spell it out at least once. Whether you spell it out and use the abbreviation in parentheses behind it, or use the abbreviation with the definition in parentheses is not important. Just give your reader a clue, at least one time.

The agency to assist you is the Abbreviated Editing Commission (AEC).

The agency to assist you is the AEC (Abbreviated Editing Commission).

Beware: A single abbreviation may have several meanings. MS, for instance, can mean millisecond, master of science, manuscript, military science, motor ship, multiple sclerosis, Mississippi or a courtesy title for a woman.

The Decimal Point

The decimal point is really a period with a pseudonym that interacts with the world of math and science. Use it in dollars and cents (The expenses amounted to $89.22) and in percentages (That paid for 25.6 percent of the trip).

Use a period when numbering an outline.

I. Grammar
   A. Words
   B. Punctuation
      1. Comma
      2. Period
      3. Parenthesis

The preferred method states that if you use a parenthesis for the numbers or letters, you may omit the period.

1. Dots
   a) Period
   b) Colon
2. Dashes
   a) hyphen
   b) long dash

But! Do not place a period after the heading itself. Refer to the above listings.

Of course, there might be one little exception. If you are listing complete sentences, then use the period at the end if you wish.

1. The chair will introduce guests.
2. Members will present voting cards.
3. The General Assembly meeting will begin.

Miscellaneous Dots

How often do you get to the end of a sentence and wonder if it is legal to use two periods? Perhaps it was this morning, about 10 A.M. You see, it is unnecessary to add a period if the sentence already ends in one (as in the abbreviation A.M.). Please note that the preceding sentence includes the abbreviation-dot inside the parenthesis and the sentence-end dot outside.

Inside/Outside? Where Do You Place Periods?

The answer is simple: Where they belong. But what if you're using other punctuation? a parenthesis? a quote mark?

Place the period at the end of a sentence. If that sentence is a quote, place it inside the quote marks.

1. Antonio blabbered, "Get the heck out of here."
2. Maria responded, "I won't 'get the heck out of here.' "
3. Her remark, "I won't get out," caused him to calm down.

In the first sentence, Antonia did all the talking.
In the second sentence, Maria talked and quoted Antonio.
In the third sentence, we are talking about what Maria said.

If the complete sentence is within the parenthesis, place the period inside. (Watch out for this one.) If the sentence is not complete within the parenthesis, place the period at the end of the sentence (and outside the closing parenthesis).

If the complete parenthetical sentence is within another complete sentence (this is a confusing idea), do not use a period inside the parenthesis.

There is one other tiny exception to "inside periods". I just used it. If the last word or words in a sentence are special terms, the period remains outside.

Picture the quoted words (above) as italics. (There is one other tiny exception to *inside periods.*) The exception rests on the difference between words which are not quoted, but words which are set apart with quote marks.

EXERCISES

(Answers to exercises are in the Appendix.)

Place commas and colons where required in the following sentences:

1. Barb began considering a vacation trip to several places Siam Australia New Zealand Fiji or New Guinea.
2. Travelers reported complimentary things about these places, such as "I was delighted with the weather as well as the "people."
3. Ken remarked "I always wanted to loaf on a tropical beach."
4. "I want to relax in the sun from about 930 in the morning to 330 in the afternoon" Barb told him.
5. "By noon the first day you'd resemble the book Bacon in the Sun with the subtitle 'Burned To a Crisp.' "

Try placing periods, commas, semicolons; you'll get the hang of it.

6. Don't try to approach a snarling beast Ken needs quiet mornings
7. Barb tries to protect him with a buffer
8. She's the buffer she screens his calls and callers
9. Another clue she likes to bring him donuts and coffee at 1000
10. When the weather turns cold she switches to hot cocoa Ken likes cocoa better than chocolate
11. She has taken to calling him by a special name Pet Hey that could be considered "petty"
12. Ken is now considering taking his bonus vacation alone all alone
13. He's looking at places like Vienna Austria Lucerne Switzerland Athens Greece Amsterdam Holland or Papeete Tahiti
14. I'd expect Barb to throw a tantrum at that one of her finest
15. Not unless they know something we don't which is possible

11

The Voices of Writing

QUESTION MARKS AND

EXCLAMATION POINTS

Question marks mark questions. What else? The problem is the placement of the mark. Is it inside or outside a quote mark? Inside or outside a parenthesis? In the middle of a sentence? All these questions will be answered in this chapter.

In the same way that question marks signal questions, exclamation points mark exclamations. Of course! Again, placement is the problem. Inside or outside the quote marks or parenthesis? We'll also address the question of when is enough too much?

QUESTION MARKS

The question mark, sometimes called an interrogation mark, is the symbol for imposing a question. It usually is placed at the end of the sentence that asks that question. Shouldn't that be simple enough?

There are a few other things you should know about the question mark. If you make a statement, then add a question at the end, use the question mark. You knew that, didn't you?

You might even pose a question without *inverting the verb and subject or using* the standard question words (who, what, why). If you want it to ask a question, use the question mark.

You did understand that?
You believe everything you hear?

Omit the question mark when making a statement that contains an indirect question.

The instructor asked if you believe everything you hear.
She asked if you understood that.

Multiple Questions and Marks

If you string several questions together with just one subject, you may use several question marks. This is the writer's choice, depending upon emphasis.

When is it right? wrong? or questionable? (correct)
When it is right, wrong or questionable? (also correct)
Will you tell me when it happened? where? and how?

Don't bother with question marks in multiple answers, however. Even if they contain the question words (who, what, when, why, how, where).
She couldn't tell me when it happened, where or how.

Placing the Question Mark

Where to put the darn thing becomes a question in itself when you get entangled with quote marks and parentheses. To determine the answer, you need to know exactly what you mean to write.

If the question is what is being quoted, the question mark belongs nestled inside the quote marks.

She asked, "Will you provide me clarification?"
Others joined in, "Will you tell us what you mean?"
Who wrote, "Why be confused?" (No, you do not need another question mark after the quote marks.)

If the whole statement is a question that just happens to include some quoted words, the question mark remains outside.

Will you clarify what you mean by "interactive behavior"?
Is what you are saying, "Interactive behavior is a good thing"?
Who wrote, "I am confused"?

The same guidelines apply to parentheses. If the question is inside, the mark must be inside also.

The instructor responded with a single question (Don't you understand?).

Why can't you get it (the idea of interactive behavior)?

If the last word of the question is an abbreviation, remember to use the
period before the question mark.

Can you turn in your report by 10 A.M.?

Would you be more comfortable working at Stateside U.?

Occasionally, rarely, once in awhile, you'll want to question something
within a statement by using a question mark in parentheses. Grammatically, it's okay to do that. But please, keep it to a minimum. Use it only
if there is no other way to express your doubt.

She claimed traffic (?) as her reason for being late.

The team won easily (?) over the opponents.

EXCLAMATION POINTS (!)

A surprise is only a surprise once. Be careful that you don't overuse the
surprise mark—the exclamation point or exclamation mark.

Used sparingly, it adds emphasis to the words you want to stand out. But
like the boy crying "Wolf!" the exclamation point is generally overused.
Watch a television commercial! Notice the wham! bang! whoopee! noises
that accompany the exclamation point on screen. After too many of them,
the impact diminishes.

The mark, used properly, expresses strong feelings, deep emotion. The
less it is used, the stronger the impact on the reader.

Consider the two following passages.

MEMO: I am disgusted! yes disgusted! with the results of last week's
sales effort. I don't even want to call it an effort! It stank! The
campaign was bad! The implementation was ineffective! The sales
people were lethargic! In short, nothing happened!!!

MEMO: I am disgusted, yes disgusted, with the results of last week's
sales effort. I don't even want to call it an effort; it stank. The
campaign was bad. The implementation was ineffective. The sales
people were lethargic. In short, nothing happened!

Strong words—disgusted, stank, ineffective, lethargic—can produce strong messages by themselves without relying on the marks. In a way, using the exclamation point properly is like the silent person who withholds comment until the right moment, then says something important— nothing happened!

Placing the Exclamation Point

Like other marks of punctuation, the placement inside or outside of quote marks or parentheses depends on the intended meaning. If the exclamation mark is inside the other marks, the exclamation is included within. If the exclamation mark is outside other marks, the whole clause becomes the exclamation.

"Don't talk to me!" the child shouted.
"Help!" the monster yelled.
I'm trying as hard as I can. (Help!)
Tell me straight out. (You're scaring me!)
What a shocking remark from a child, "I feel invisible"!
So much anguish from the single word "help"!
What a scary production (Beauty and the Beast)!

EXERCISES
(Answers to exercises are in the Appendix.)

Place appropriate commas, periods, question or exclamation marks in the following sentences.

1. Why would they want to throw us off with their antics
2. Why indeed is my comment
3. Never add unnecessary words to a sentence never
4. Surely that bothers you doesn't it
5. You bet it does
6. If we wait will their antics change
7. Obviously you haven't seen the movie "The Art of Being Artful"
8. Where oh where can I find a video tape copy
9. Ken and Barb will be back from their vacations soon anyway
10. Then of course we'll have the answers to where what why and whatever won't we

12

Enclosures of the Word Kind

PARENTHESIS, BRACKETS AND

QUOTATION MARKS

Often discounted as unimportant, the parenthesis and brackets can add or detract from a piece of writing. 1) Use parens (acceptable abbreviation) to enclose disconnected elements that you want to de-emphasize. 2) Use them to insert an aside (please avoid ha-ha). 3) Use them to clarify legal figures that follow the spelled out number. 4) Use them to enclose a series of numbers or letters that introduce narrative lists. (Some punctuationists are adamant about including both fore and aft parens with numbers. Some prefer just the aft.)

Brackets are used in academic and technical writing. They will enclose words added by an author in the midst of quoting another author, something like an editorial note. They're sometimes used to set off a parenthesis within a parenthesis.

While it may seem obvious to use quotation marks to set off words that are quoted, there are questions about where to place the marks, when to use them and how often to use them. Do the quote marks go before or after the period, question mark, exclamation mark? This offers a good place to review other associated quandaries. Are there two periods at the end of a sentence that closes with an abbreviation such as A.M.? Never. We'll also discuss long quotes, indirect quotes and quotes within quotes.

The word processor and its ability to emulate typesetting rules has changed some of the grammar rules. This is one of them. With a typewriter, it is necessary to underscore titles of major works and unconventional words. With word processing, we can use italics easily. The quote marks are still used, however, for titles of minor works.

PARENTHESIS ( )

The parenthesis is an enclosed expression that you feel important enough to be included, but not important enough to hold its own in a sentence. Sometimes this information explains or defines. Sometimes it comments. The word "parenthesis" refers to the expression and one or both of the marks that enclose such an expression. Since the marks are usually used in pairs, the word parenthesis (singular) is appropriate. The plural (parentheses) is used to refer to multiple parenthetical expressions and to both of the parenthesis marks. This is similar to the use of "ellipsis."

Within another sentence, the parenthetical expression does not call for capital letter beginnings nor period endings.

The storm hit at mid-day (right in the middle of lunch hour) and caused considerable damage.

When the parenthetical words come within a sentence that requires a comma or other punctuation, place the comma after the closing parenthesis.

The rain descended in torrents (it was a devastating experience), flooding the streets.

When making references, do not capitalize the referring word *see*.

Damage was extensive (see the evening newspaper) throughout the city.

In the following example, the question mark points to the question within the parentheses; the period marks the end of the sentence.

I visited Rainville during the last storm in May (or was it April?).

If the parenthetical information is given its own sentence, it is written as a regular sentence within the parentheses. (This is fairly simple to understand.)

The storm continued for hours. (My own house remained undamaged.) The entire city lost electrical power.

Numbers and letters

The parenthesis sets aside numbers and letters when used to list a series of ideas or things, or when outlining. This can be done in a number of ways. Simplification in today's business world encourages a single parenthesis instead of both. Just be consistent in which choice you make.

The plan called for (1) a committee to be named, (2) a visit to the site, and (3) affirmation by the entire council.

The following example uses the single parens:

The plan:
1) Name a committee
2) Visit the site
3) Take it to the council

Formal/legal parenthesis

In formal writing, usually in connection with legal documents, the parenthesis is used to clarify information:

The Party of the First Part (Adam J. Stone) and the Party of the Second Part (Eve G. Garden) enter into this agreement.
The amount paid in compensation amounted to Thirty Thousand Dollars ($30,000.00), to be paid in one lump sum.
(Note that legal folk love to add the zeros in the cents column. They usually aren't necessary.)

Parenthesis as de-emphasis

In many of the above examples, the parenthetical information could have been set aside with commas or dashes. By placing the information in parenthesis, the writer is playing down its importance. In Chapter 13, you'll see how dashes set off information, play it up, emphasize it. Choose your strategy and use the appropriate marks.

Notice the difference:

1. You may receive this offer for a small amount—only $9.95—for a limited time only.
2. You may receive this offer for a small amount (only $9.95) for a limited time only.

You'd want to use the first if this is a for-real bargain. Let's say it is an article you usually would pay twice the amount to own.

However, if this is a gadget worth a much smaller amount, you'd want to play it down, place it in parenthesis, as in the second sentence. If you feel so-so about it, you may choose to set off the price with commas. This tidbit of information on the psychological effects of punctuation is particularly useful in preparing sales messages of any kind (see Chapter 20).

BRACKETS [ ]

No, brackets are not just square parentheses. They have some uses all their very own.

Use brackets when you have a parenthetical remark within another parenthetical remark.

Trees such as these are found in warm climates (in North and South Carolina, Georgia and Alabama [especially the Gulf Coast region] and in Florida).

Timber from these trees is particularly long-lasting. (Some suggest even longer-lasting than mahogany [see page 35] when used in furniture.)

Brackets are useful in setting apart the comments of one writer when quoting another.

Employees at the saw mill stated in their request, "We want everyone to know that Arnie [Line Supervisor Arnold R. Matson] has agreed with our need for a new saw."

"This group wants to request $15,000 [that figure has since been reduced to $12,000] for new equipment."

Brackets for *Sic*

When quoting a piece of writing or a spoken statement, it is necessary to repeat it exactly as written or spoken. Occasionally, there will be words that are misspelled or misstated that you may want to note as such. The way to do that is to write the Latin word *sic* and place it in brackets behind the misquote. That tells the world that you are only copying as delivered.

The class sang, "Row, row, row your coat [sic], gently down the stream."

"Tell me, Josiph [sic], do you care about me?" she wrote on her lilac stationery.

Without the bracketed *sic*, you run the risk of having words corrected by an editor, or having your knowledge questioned as a writer.

> People who live in Tacoma, Washington, and attend Tahoma [sic] High School know what this means.

Quotation Marks " "

Quotation marks come in pairs, an open quote and a close quote. They also come in sets of singles and doubles. They resemble uplifted commas, except that they can also appear upside-down. Open quotes look like upside down commas. Close quotes look like rightside-up commas. On the typewriter, there is no such distinction because the inch mark (") is used for quotations. In typeset copy, there is a distinct difference.

Quotation marks are used to set off quoted material. No surprise there. They usually are reserved for the exact words.

> Mandy told her client, "I can't work any faster."
> The client retorted, "I have an appointment in exactly 30 minutes."
> "My work demands plenty of time," Mandy came back, "and requires you to sit still."

Punctuation in all of the above examples is placed inside the quotation marks. There are a few exceptions.

> Mandy was saying, "I have to take my time"; the client was responding, "I don't have time." (Notice the semicolon is outside the quotes. Use only punctuation pertaining to the quoted material inside the marks.)

A quotation does not have to be the entire sentence. There will be times you'll want to use only a few words. Use quotation marks around the quoted section only.

> Mandy repeatedly told the client she needed to "take my time" and be patient.

In normal written dialog, each speaker receives a new paragraph. Notice in novels how you can follow the conversation without the speaker being mentioned each time it changes. In business correspondence (minutes, legal proceedings, report writing), this guideline is followed.

Supervisor Teton spoke first. "I am the boss in this factory," he said.
"And I am a respected employee," Jamey spoke back.
"When I give an order, I expect it to be carried out."
"I did that," responded Jamey, "and I carried it out right down the line.
  I don't see what this fuss is all about anyway." Jamey turned his back
  at this point and appeared to walk away.

As long as one speaker is continuing, or as long as you are writing about that speaker, keep it in the same paragraph.
Do not use quote marks if you are not quoting.

She asked the question, Is anyone right?
He answered with a simple no.

Single Quote Marks

Sometimes you'll find a quote within a quote.

Perry offered, "I'll tell you right now that she said, 'I want to go along.'
  Those were her exact words: 'I want to go along.' "

Use the single quote within another quote. And don't forget to close them both at the proper place. Always close the single quote first.
Yes, if there is a quote within a quote within a quote, you return to the double quote marks. But please try to avoid this kind of confusion. Writing, by its very form of words on paper, is difficult enough to translate without adding further confusion about who is saying what.

Alternative Quotation Procedures

Long quotations can be handled in several ways. One is to maintain the same type style and continue quoting. In this case, begin each new paragraph with open-quote marks. Do not use close quotes until the end of the final paragraph. The open quote marks tell the reader that the quotation continues. Don't disappoint them before the end.
Long quotations can be set in a different type style. The material may be indented, single spaced, or bold-faced. In this case, you won't need any quotation marks at all. The type change tells the reader this is a quote. This kind of change is particularly effective when quoting newspaper articles or information from a report. Credit for the quote can be given either at the outset or in a line by itself at the close.

MADISON, WI September 1, 1979—Citizens of the city were shocked this morning to learn a large section of Madison was doomed to be torn down.

Righteously up in arms, the townspeople are preparing today to march on the State Capitol, challenging the right of the City to destroy history.

Legislative Representative Leona Morgan told the crowd, "I know nothing of this transgression, but I will look into it."

The angry crowd is expected to stage a major protest march on Saturday night, moving to the rotunda to confront the Legislature.

—State Newspaper, September 1, 1979

Special Words

Sometimes a writer uses quotation marks to express special meaning to words. Slang, coined words and euphemisms are so treated.

The pilot was careful to note the location of his "little black box."

When the plane took off for the first time, the navigator, "a greenhorn," shouted with glee.

We have to note in the records that these "changing times" are killing our budget process.

It's impossible to hire any more "account executives" when what we need are salespeople!

Along with word processors now comes the ability to italicize words easily. In typewritten messages, special words are underlined for emphasis. With word processing, the words are italicized. Translate underline into italicize.

Some quoted words may read better as *italics*. Technical words, for instance, when used in conventional texts, should be used with either quote marks or italics.

The Board of Directors was asked to provide "attitudinal neutralization equipment" throughout the office, meaning the office staff needs more coffee machines.

By using both techniques in one sentence, the quote mark tone suggests that somebody is playing with somebody's head when they could have spoken more clearly in the beginning.

Titles of Newspapers, Books, Magazines, Etc.

Here's one that Miss Miller told you about that you promptly dismissed from your mind. You've probably been wondering ever since how to write the title of a book as opposed to the title of a magazine article. Do we underline? italicize? quote?

Whole works (books, magazines, newspapers, long musical works, plays) are italicized in print. When typing them, use the underline method or all capital letters. When printing, use italics.

Type: My favorite novel is Gone With the Wind.
Or: My favorite novel is GONE WITH THE WIND.
Print (Word Processing): My favorite novel is *Gone With the Wind*.

Short works (parts of longer works such as chapters, articles, news items, short stories, songs, one-act plays, poems) are written with quotation marks.

I enjoyed your article, "How To Write With Your Left Hand," as printed in *Livelihood Magazine*.
The news item, headed "Left-hand writing is tough," caught my eye in today's *Sun/Moon Times*.
You ought to write a song, "Write Left-handed and Cry."

EXERCISES
(Answers to exercises are in the Appendix)

Insert enclosures (parenthesis, brackets, quotation marks) where they are needed:

1. I found a copy of that video The Art of Being Artful.
2. Did it provide clues to our friends' behavior? asked Elizabeth.
3. Tony responded, No, not a bit.
4. My postcard from Tahiti simply said, Having a gooood her word time, glad you're not here.
5. Tony was speechless a rare experience for him.
6. Let's list the facts: 1 Ken and Barbara are both on vacation. 2 They both headed for the South Pacific. 3 We've had only one postcard from Barb.
7. The conclusion shades of Sherlock Holmes is they must be together.
8. We don't know that, Tony found his voice.
9. Look, the postcard has a P.S. Jeanette interjected. It says Tahihi sic is terrific. KP.
10. That says it all. Elizabeth smiled and returned to her office. She knows more than she's telling, said Jeanette.

13

Dots and Dashes

APOSTROPHES, ELLIPSIS, HYPHENS,
DASHES, AND DIAGONALS

The little raised dot-with-a-tail, called the *apostrophe*, combined with the word *its*, raises more havoc in written communication than any other mark. When do you insert it and when do you not? Here is a review of possessives and contractions; these are the places that apostrophes are used. They are also the places that apostrophes are misused. An apostrophe is used to indicate omission of letters or numbers, some of which result in contractions. An apostrophe may be used to form the plural of a number, letter, symbol, or certain abbreviations. Notice the conditional verb *may*. This is the writer's choice.

The *ellipsis* is a lesser known mark with a single use. The three little dots mean only that something is missing . . . such as part of a quote.

Hyphens are used to divide words, for one purpose or another. Sometimes they're used in compound adjectives, and sometimes they divide words between syllables at the end of a line (an art in itself).

Dashes have lives of their own, not connected with hyphens. The dash is more powerful and is used to set off expressions you want to emphasize. It is used before a summary set of words, to indicate an afterthought, to set off an interruption clause, and before a word or phrase that is repeated for emphasis. The dash is used before the name of an author or a work that follows a direct quotation. And the dash is used before an introductory expression such as *for example* if the words following are to be emphasized.

Diagonals offer the reader choices. They're sometimes used to replace the word *or*. The diagonal can divide words that are similar or opposites, allowing the reader to decide which to select.

THE APOSTROPHE (')

The apostrophe has a few varied uses that don't produce much of a pattern. The high-strung, elevated comma is used as a single quote mark (a quote within a quote), to form possessives, to form contractions (they fill a spot where a letter or letters have been removed), and on certain occasions, to form a plural (with numbers, letters, and other symbols).

Please refer to Chapter 1, where the apostrophe is used to show possession, and to Chapter 2, where it is not used to show possession.

Noun Possessives

Add an apostrophe s ('s) or single apostrophe (') to nouns to indicate possession.

The city manager's division was in a turmoil.
The civic leaders' dinner was an event of its own.

Pronoun Possessives

Do not use an apostrophe in personal possessive pronouns (hers, theirs, its, ours, yours) found in Column C (See Chapter 2).

Its main consideration was the cities' electrical power.
The distraught council confused ownership: theirs, yours and ours.
However, the problem was theirs, not the committee's.

Use the apostrophe with the other pronouns, that is, the ones that don't look like pronouns: one, another, somebody, someone, anyone, anybody.

She selected one scarf's color and another's size to use in her new
    creation.
It was anybody's guess as to what to call its new form.

Plural Possessives

Some people think that s-ending, pluralized possessive words should have yet another apostrophe s at the end. (You decide.)

The Morrises' names kept getting mixed up.
The Morrises's names kept getting mixed up.

Contractions

Writing a sentence without contractions can appear formal and is not the way someone would speak the words. Contractions appear less formal, and make reading (and often, understanding) easier. To form a contraction, use the apostrophe to hold open the space where the letter or letters are removed.

Don't = do not
Can't = cannot
Won't = will not
Shouldn't = should not
He's = he is
There's = there is

A designer *cannot* understand why *it is* important to conduct analysis sessions that *will not* be too long.

A designer *can't* understand why *it's* important to conduct analysis sessions that *won't* be too long.

The same guidelines apply to any number or letter that may be removed: In the '50s (instead of 1950s), banks seldom opened before 10 o'clock (of the clock).

Numbers and Letters

The apostrophe is used to help readers identify plurals of numbers and letters. Such use is completely optional. Use it or not.

Mind your *p's* and *q's*.
This was a saying in the *1920's*.
Be careful about using too many *even's* in your written copy.
These are powerful *do's* and *don'ts* in good writing.

Wait a minute, you say. You just wrote the '50s without an apostrophe before the *s* (above). Right. Sometimes the apostrophe can be overused. The mark is usually omitted except where it is absolutely necessary to clarify meaning. We could have written: '50's or don't's. Two apostrophes in one word is over-use; no apostrophes may be confusing. (If we write dos and donts, the reader would have to pause to grasp the meaning.) Moderation, as Miss Miller used to say. Moderation in all things, including the use of apostrophes.

Apostrophe in Measurements

In technical writing, the apostrophe may be used to represent measurement in feet: The room was 9' × 12'. (The carpet fit a 9-foot by 12-foot room.)

Footnotes on Apostrophes

Clever ads get our attention. And advertisers know the value of proper punctuation.

A clever company named Saturday's Wearables used the apostrophe to promote its products. A giant billboard read: Saturday's Are For What?

An advertiser named Gai's wanted customers to recognize its name. It produced a commercial with a little girl spelling out the company name in her childish sing-song voice. She had to mispronounce the word apostrophe to keep up the cadence of the jingle. She spelled: G-A-I-APOS-TER-OPHEE-S. It worked. No one is likely to misspell the name.

THE ELLIPSIS (. . .)

Three little dots in a row are considered an ellipsis, which comes from a Greek word meaning to fall short or leave out. The ellipsis (singular word) indicates that something is being omitted, whether it is in the beginning, middle or end of a sentence. An alternative symbol of the ellipsis is a triple asterisk (***).

The nominating chair spoke at length ". . . to present a slate of new officers that will be . . . acceptable to the entire assembly . . ." Her words began, "It is my honor to . . . ." If the ellipsis ends the sentence, the fourth dot (a period) is added.

A word about technology. As word processors replace typewriters, new skills in using them affect both the way we type and the way the product prints out. Most word processing programs contain a separate key for the ellipsis. Check yours to see how to make all three dots show up simultaneously.

THE HYPHEN (-)

The hyphen is called an n-dash by typesetters because its width is the same as the letter n. A hyphen separates words or parts of words to avoid confusion.

The Hyphen (In Compound Words)

The evolution of compound words (a single new word made up of two or more individual words) once took years to complete. Now, new compound words seem to appear overnight. You can tell a person's age by asking them to spell brownbag, as in lunch. If they spell it as two words, they're probably over 50. If they use a hyphen, they are baby boomers in their 40s. If they spell it as one word, they learned it in the last 30 years.

That's what happens to compound words. They begin as two words (usually nouns) and are used together often enough to slide into one word.

Yes, there's a guideline for knowing when to hyphen and when not to hyphen. If the first part of the compound word has a single syllable, write both parts as one word (as long as it is easily understood).

The following nouns began as separate words, then were hyphenated for a time before becoming single words.

Bookkeeper	Taxpayer
Boombox	Textbook
Bedroom	Teenager
Homemaker	Househusband

If the first part has more than one syllable, use a hyphen, or separate the words without using a hyphen.

Baby boomers	Baby-sit
Kitty litter	Doggy bag
Managing director	Account executive

This is a guideline, not a hard-and-fast rule. The only way to be sure about some compound words is to consult a good dictionary. The word *pastime* is often misspelled as *past-time*. The title of vice president does not include a hyphen (unless the title represents the president of vice). You may hyphenate vice-regent, vice-chancellor and vice-consul, but not vice president.

The Hyphen (With Adjectives)

Sometimes several adjectives are used to modify a noun. If all of them can apply directly to the noun, commas are used to separate them.

The job applicant was friendly, witty, energetic and skilled.
She also had curly, brown hair and bright, blue eyes.

The commas used in the second sentence could have been omitted, and the sentence would remain clear.

She also had curly brown hair and bright blue eyes.

The hyphen is used mostly to indicate compound adjectives. When other modifiers are used to form compound adjectives, the hyphen is the only little mark that stands between confusion (sometimes catastrophic, sometimes just silly) and understanding. The clue is the way the other modifiers cannot relate directly to the noun, only to the other adjective(s).

Where could hyphens be placed in the following sentences to make sense?

The second hand painted bowl sold for $358.
That $11,000 figure represented the small car sale price.
The team won the pennant with an extra base hit.
Four architects submitted small scale designs.
The judges' bigger is better decision was instantly apparent.

By adding hyphens, we tell the reader that certain words go together, and certain ones do not.

The second-hand painted bowl sold for $358.
Or
The second hand-painted bowl sold for $358.
That $11,000 figure represented the small-car sale price.
Or
That $11,000 figure represented the small car-sale price.
The team won the pennant with an extra base hit.
Or
The team won the pennant with an extra-base hit.
Four architects submitted small-scale designs.
Or
Four architects submitted small scale-designs.
The judges' bigger-is-better decision was instantly apparent.

If the hyphenated adjective combinations are placed after the nouns they modify, the hyphen is omitted.

The bowl was hand painted.
The architects submitted designs that were on a small scale.

The Hyphen (With Participles)

At the risk of getting into technicalities, there is a guideline that might help make decisions about when to use and when not to use the hyphen. Remember when we talked about the verbal participle, we indicated it could function as an adjective? This is the place.

When one element of a compound modifier is a participle (*ing* or *ed* added onto a verb form), a hyphen must be used.

However expensive, that is a *good-looking* car.
The driver is grabbing a *much-needed* rest.
Let him remain a *not-awake* dozer, since he may not be a *law-abiding* citizen.
We've rehearsed this *fine-tuned* drill a thousand times.

If you re-read these sentences without the hyphen, they may make no sense at all the first time. The hyphen says the words have to be used together.

Here's the helpful guideline: if the participle is modified by an adverb ending in *ly*, you won't need the hyphen. It will be a perfectly clear statement.

Hers was a finely tuned classic car.
The driver grabbed a sorely needed rest.
Let him remain a barely awake dozer, since he may not be a law-abiding citizen.
We've rehearsed this finely tuned drill a thousand times.

Guidelines to use or not to use a hyphen in a two-or-more-word modifier:

1. Check to see if one of the words is a participle (*ing* or *ed* verb form). If it is, use the hyphen.
2. Check to see if the word modifying the participle ends in *ly*. If it does, leave out the hyphen. If it doesn't, put the hyphen in.

Short form: If you read the sentence and it is perfectly clear without the hyphen, leave it out. If you had to pause to be sure how to read it, put the hyphen in.

The Hyphen (With Verbs and Prepositions)

When verbs and prepositions are combined to make a single-meaning, they can either be one word or a hyphenated word. Here again, you need to decide if the words written as one make an understandable new word, or a jumble.

takeover
tipoff
dropout
putdown

But:

put-on
come-on
get-up
tie-off

If the last four were spelled together, they would read: puton, comeon, getup, tieup. This would make the reader work hard.

Warning: When using these same words as a verb and preposition, do not use a hyphen. Write them this way:

take over	put on
tip off	come on
drop out	get up
put down	tie up

If the members take over the gym, it is not necessarily referred to as a takeover.

If new players come on the floor, it is not necessarily a come-on.

The Hyphen (With Prefixes)

A good dictionary is a must for making sure about these words. Most dictionaries carry inset columns of words using common prefixes (word beginnings): *co, in, over, pre, re, un.*

Here are a few guidelines:

Co before a noun usually is hyphenated: co-counsel, co-author, co-chair, co-star (noun). But put *co* in front of a verb and they may run together: cooperate, coordinate, costar (verb).

Self generally takes a hyphen when it is used as a prefix: self-evident, self-centered, self-esteem, self-explanatory. Some exceptions include selfsame, selfish, selfhood, selfless (each is one word).

Anti gets along without a hyphen except when it is followed by a root word beginning with *i* (anti-inflation, anti-inflammatory) or when it is followed by a proper noun (anti-Communism, anti-Capitalism, anti-West).

When using *re* as a prefix, use a hyphen if it means to do something again: re-finish, re-start, re-type, re-state. Do not use a hyphen in words such as renew, renovate, remake. This may help to understand the difference between remark and re-mark. Again, use the dictionary.

Because *ex* has its own meaning (it is its own word on occasion, as in *I want you to meet my ex*), use a hyphen to indicate something former: ex-partner, ex-soldier, ex-star. Miss Miller reminded us that *ex* isn't dignified enough for some positions. We need to use *former* when discussing has-beens in rarified fields: former president, former chief of staff, former secretary of state.

Some suffixes (word endings) also take a hyphen. When words like *emeritus* or *elect* follow a title, they are hyphenated: president-elect, director-emeritus.

When more than one word is connected to a prefix, the hyphen is used at the end of each prefix: three- and five-year leases; pro- and anti-choice; semi- and full-circle events.

The Hyphen (As Word Connector)

The hyphen is used to connect two words that are joined to form a new idea, usually proper names. In a time when women are retaining their family names by joining them to their husband's family name, the hyphenated name is taking on great popularity.

Hyphens are used in some trade names (Alka-Seltzer, Alpha-Bits) and family names (Smith-Warner, Thompson-Hobbs).

The hyphen also joins number words: (twenty-two, fifty-seven), fractions (three-fourths, one-half), numerals to other units of measurement (6-foot ladder, 2,000-year-old man), and written numbers to dollar amounts (eight-thousand seven-hundred twenty-five dollars).

The Hyphen (As Word Divider)

The hyphen separates words at the end of a line that must be divided in order to fit the type setting. (This is becoming a lost art as computers take over this function.)

Miss Miller's class called it syllabification (proudly displaying this new long word). It means to divide words according to syllables, so if one doesn't quite fit at the end of a line, some of it can be placed on the following line. A few rules will help (they aren't very important now that computers already know all of them by heart).

The prime rule is to follow common sense. Use the division as far into the word as you can: (investiga tion, impracti cal); don't divide abbreviations or combinations of numerals; don't divide one-syllable words; divide between syllables (repeat the word out loud if you have to); avoid leaving one or two letters on a line (un necessary, agend a); avoid ending more than two consecutive lines with hyphens; avoid dividing proper names; and never leave a hyphen at the end of a page.

Divide words between double consonants (unneces sary).

Divide words between the root word and the ending (begin ning).

Do not divide before a vowel that makes up its own syllable (infatua tion, initi ate). If the one-letter syllable is part of a recognized suffix, keep the suffix together (poss ible, incap able).

Divide hyphenated words only at the hyphen (first-rate).

When in doubt, look at a good dictionary. Words are written in obvious syllables.

If you rely on a computer, re-check a printout of the copy for too many hyphenated words. These can easily be changed by placing a return in front of the hyphenated word. The wrap effect of the computer automatically carries the word to the next line. Some programs allow you to turn off the automatic hyphen, thus avoiding all word breakups.

The Hyphen (As Speller)

The hyphen is used to indicate a spelled-out word: Please tell the truth, the whole truth, the t-r-u-t-h.

THE DASH (—)

If the hyphen is an n-dash, the bona fide long dash is called an m-dash. That is, it is twice as long as the hyphen. The typist, therefore, uses two hyphens to equal a dash. The word processor has a special key to produce this useful punctuation mark. Debates abound on the subject of whether or not to place spaces before and after the dash. Most professional printers do not use spaces.

Occasionally, an expression that you might consider placing in parenthesis will do a better job following a dash—just for emphasis. As the parenthesis diminishes an idea, the dash augments it, plays it up.

> The bowling team—you know who they are—plays on Thursday nights.
> Come and watch the team—especially Sidearm Johnson—do their stuff.

A definitive phrase following a noun is sometimes—not always—set off with dashes. Dashes are especially useful when the definition contains commas of its own:

> Four members of the team—Davenport, Downing, Davidson, and Denver—showed up for practice.

The dash is helpful too in summing up a preceding series.

> Gutter balls, line errors, dropped balls—all of these are problems that need correction.

The dash may indicate an afterthought—if that is relevant.
Emphasize a word by repeating it after a dash.

> The outcome was successful—successful in that the other team didn't show up.

The dash sometimes replaces the colon in introducing an expression. The words following the dash are such words as *for instance*, or *namely*.

> We'll try to raise another team—for instance, in about ten years.

The dash is often used as a credit for a long quote. The dash precedes the name of the author or the publication being quoted.

> "Good words are worth much and cost little."—George Herbert.

Like the exclamation point, dashes can be overdone. Generally, a good comma will do the same thing as a dash. Use the dash with care—when to do so would be most effective.

THE DIAGONAL, OR VIRGULE (/)

The comma, you remember, is often used to replace the word *and*. In the same way, the slanted diagonal mark is used to replace the word *or*. Sometimes called a *virgule* (there's a word to toss off at the next office meeting!), it is placed between words that show alternatives, sometimes opposites.

Your lunch consists of sandwich, coffee, soup and/or salad.
Notice this is not an either/or choice, but an and/or.
They want to appeal to your physical/emotional senses.
The religious/scientific implications are best left to the experts.

The diagonal/virgule also indicates relativity, replacing the word per.

The space ship traveled at 2,500 miles/hour.
Using the formula, the tapestry contains 846 stitches/inch.

You'll notice that the examples used here do not reflect a choice of his/her. This attempt to avoid sexism is awkward in the least and not half as effective as the alternatives (see Chapter 21).

EXERCISES
(Answers to exercises are in the Appendix.)

Place apostrophes, hyphens and dashes where they are needed:

1. In a weeks time, Barb and Ken returned sun tanned to their office.
2. You could see the vacations effect on them both.
3. Barbara dove into her stacked up work; Ken began calling on badly neglected clients.
4. Its evident they missed their work.
5. Its also evident they didn't miss its concentration.
6. Where else could they get a tan like that the Caribbean?
7. Everyone missed having them around the bickering, in fighting, double entendres.
8. "Lets get some work done around here," suggested James the boss.
9. "We need a new campaign for the ultra new Banks account one of the most over sold, under publicized accounts in the country," James challenged them.

10. "Theyre eager to see what well come up with," he added.
11. Separate the following words into syllables appropriate for hyphenation:

accommodation
merriment
satisfaction
security
right
account
safety
reliability
convenience
bankers

Part 3

CREATING YOUR
OWN STYLE

Some people would think twice about going to a party in their work clothes, or to work in their party clothes because of the impression they want to make. Other people consider clothes as a means of expressing themselves. (Go to any mall and watch the teenagers.) Appearance is important.

Writers express themselves and make impressions with their words. Like teenagers, you're making impressions whether you're trying or not. "Look at this." "Watch me." "This isn't important." "I don't care." "I care a lot."

Making the impression you want to make is the subject of this part.

To make the right impression, you first need to know what kind of impression you want. Do you want to come off as flamboyant? conservative? venturesome? reliable? Advertisers know the value of image in presenting themselves to the public. The same holds true for writers presenting themselves to a single reader or millions of readers.

Perhaps the best way to discuss image is to become aware of the image presented by others. Read a piece of writing and consider how much it tells about the person who wrote it. Look at the choice of words, the structure of the sentences, the length and construction of the paragraphs. Is this writer an educated person? Are the words spelled right? Does this writer care about appearance? Is this writer male or female, and what are the feelings about sexist language? Does the writer have a grasp of how to use the American language?

Look closely. Does the writer feel comfortable with the words, or hemmed in by rules? Are the ideas clear and easily followed? Can you get into the writer's mind and know what kind of person lives there?

Like composing a song, we'll look first for the words, then add the music. Structuring sentences and building paragraphs are like adding the instruments to the piano composition—just the right amount with just the right intensity.

You'll pick up four ways to improve your spelling, so simple you'll start recognizing misspelled words. You may even begin grinding your teeth over misspelled words on readerboards.

Those illusive numbers and ways to use them in business correspondence is the topic of one chapter. Writing nonsexist language (without overdoing the he/she or the person words) is another chapter subject.

Then you'll discover a variety of ways to style an individual composition. Are you simply relaying information? Do you have a negative message to impart? Do you want someone to come around to your way of thinking? In other words, why are you writing this piece and have you chosen the best format?

Writing with a purpose is as important as knowing the destination of a journey before you start out. Aiming your message is as simple as aiming your car in the right direction. Are you planning to impress, inform, or inquire? Do you need to document? Who will read this message? Friend? Competitor? Boss?

Writing persuasively is a challenge that can be put to use every day. Whether you're selling yourself as a spouse, parent, professional, hard worker, knowledgeable expert, or just a nice person, you need to have some guidelines for writing persuasively.

All this and more is the subject of this part. You should find it helpful in applying all the preceding grammar and punctuation guidelines. Now it's time to put it all together.

14

Words—Troublesome, New, Wonderful

The primary components of writing are words, obviously. So obvious, in fact, we forget to consider them as important components. In this chapter we'll consider the way language changes as word usage changes within the culture. And why not make up a word with a specific meaning just for you and your communicatees? (There, I just made up one!) Words are wonderful, aren't they. You'll never look at them again as just components.

If words are the material of communication, then grammar is the tool to use them. Like most tools, they are meant to shape and fine-tune the material, not only in standard uses, but in creative ways. Please don't be afraid of words. Get to know them, their wide ranges, their possibilities, as well as their dictionary meanings. You can even make up some yourself.

The dictionary is another tool, but only a part of the tool set. If word usage were restricted to dictionary definitions, we'd end up speaking like newcomers to the American language—using single words to express needs and little else (me eat, you wait). The dictionary is only a guide, offering basic meanings, pronunciation, root derivations, grammar functions and, sometimes, examples of usage. The rest is up to you.

Most United States dictionaries use English as a language base. They trace words to origins, dating them and locating where they came from. Dictionary prefaces are full of information about words and language. Read them and be impressed with how much is known about words.

Dictionaries judge words too. Words are labelled according to their acceptance in polite society (and academia). You'll find dictionaries attach such labels as *dialect, slang, idiom, postulate, substandard, obsolete* and *archaic*. Look up the same word in another dictionary and you'll find that various editors differ on which words belong with which labels. How long does it take for a word to go from idiom or slang to obsolete and archaic?

The thesaurus is another tool for word users. Such a book offers shades of meanings to words. Where the dictionary provides denotative meanings, the basics, a thesaurus offers connotative meanings, the side issues. Ask a half dozen people for their definitions of a word like *peace*, and you'll receive half a dozen variations of the dictionary meanings. Finding those variations is the work of the thesaurus.

Since we're talking about tools, let's talk about the tools of the writer: the typewriter. No, that's not exactly accurate. When the machine was invented, the word *typewriter* was given to the person operating the machine, now called the *typist*. Almost a century later, the verb *to type* is giving way to another new verb, *to keyboard*. This new verb use for the old noun—keyboarding—developed probably because men were averse to typing and the prolific nature of the computer made it necessary for both women and men in business to type. What is most ironic is the full circle of the word meanings. Where once men were the typewriters, then women became typists, now computer users (men and women) spend their days keyboarding.

Most computers also bring with them spelling and grammar checks programs. They are great for catching the obvious errors, but please don't depend on them. After all, you're smarter than that computer program! It fails at times and offers such messages as "can't find" or "no such word." You don't have to accept that message as final. Read on.

PLAYING WITH WORDS

Different people use words in different ways. Word artists (poets, fiction writers, advertising writers) play with words, expand them, squeeze them, misspell them, pile multiple meanings on top of one another, and change word functions.

Many of the new verbs beginning to appear in the dictionary are the result of an ad copy writer's whim. Where else could we have found the verb *prioritize* that came from the noun *priority*? Creative spelling and word usage once came only from poets who liked to rhyme words that were similarly spelled, and vice-versa. Now ad writers creatively spell words to fit their sounds: lite, enuf, nite, tuff.

One day (this is a prediction) the current word *light* will be universally (in the dictionary) spelled *lite*. There are several reasons for this prediction. First of all, it's easy. Secondly, it makes sense. Finally, the word is appearing in all the places that people look for spelling hints—on television and on their food.

Night might make it to *nite* about the same time, and *tight* one day might become *tite*. But don't look for *right*, *sight*, or *might* to change spellings, because the words *rite*, *site* and *mite* have other meanings all their own.

If you can't find the word in the dictionary, make it up. You probably never heard Miss Miller give this advice. (More likely, she told you that if it isn't in the dictionary, it isn't a word.) We know, however, that unlike the chicken and egg scam that's been going on for years, the dictionary did not come before the word. It came after, and it still does. "In the beginning there was the word." Remember?

MAKE UP YOUR OWN

How do you make up a word? Actually, there are two ways. One is the way most words are devised, by finding a root word and altering it. Another way is to find two or more words that belong together and combine them.

Let's say you need a noun to show what happens when someone tells a funny story about politics. *Funny story* or *joke* doesn't quite fit the bill. You want a word that defines the kind of story as well as the way it is told. You try *political humor*, *politico-comedy*, *politico-joke*, *joke-politico*! Not quite. You want the essence of story in there. Look up politics in the dictionary. Learn that the root comes from *the people*, *the government*. Look up adjoining combinations of words: politicalize, politicize (politisighs), politick (from the noun politicking). Now there's a word to play with. *Politick*, *politrick*, *politruck*. Check the thesaurus and find alternatives for story (tale, plot). Put them together and come up with *politale*. Not bad for a first try.

More likely, new words come from what feels natural. It's one of those there-oughta-be-a-word experiences. One author writing about a society where women and men share equal standing has come up with the word *equalitarian*. It plays off the word *egalitarian* from a French word which means the same thing. But this author uses a spelling that comes closer to the exact meaning she wishes to imply.

Hey, communicator. You can do that too. There's no law that if you find a better word, or a better combination of words, that you can't share it with other communicators. If they like it, they'll use it. And possibly, one day a dictionary will print it. If no one else likes it, the word will come to a natural and expected demise.

A friend with a new home has made a quasi-pet out of the squirrel that plays in her yard. She calls it her *yard-squirrel*. While the term isn't in the dictionary, it adequately describes the animal.

Here are some familiar words you may recognize: *doozie* (it's in the dictionary), *intersomnambulists*—people who dream the same dreams (not in the dictionary), *wannabe*—a hopeful copy-cat; *bungee jumping*— a new recreation.

Be assured that when you use words in a new way, someone will caution you about following the dictionary. Do you remember Miss Miller proclaiming, "You can't use *ain't* because it isn't in the dictionary!"? When that happens, just ask them if they understood what you wrote. If they did, congratulations! You have coined a new word.

Words are fascinating when you take a close look at them. There are many words that sound alike but have several spellings and meanings (wise/whys, whose/who's, reel/real, pair/pear, bare/bear, roll/role). There are words that are spelled alike, but have different meanings (put, take, up, shade, flower, monitor, jack-ass). There are words that have a variety of meanings according to the way they are pronounced (record, produce, progress, project, polish).

TECHNICAL LANGUAGE (LANGUAGE OF THE FIELD)

Legal people use words in almost a backward way. They go to the dictionary as the authority for word meanings, build sentences with words that are made to fit together according to the rules, and squeeze more long words into long sentences than any document should be made to bear. That is part of practicing law. (Interesting use of the word *practice*.)

Don't blame the lawyers. Vague, multi-meaning duplicitous words are the language of the law. In other words, that is the attorneys' technical language.

Every field of endeavor has its own technical language. Put a sports writer with a military strategist and they might understand one another because their technical languages borrow from each other. But put a sports writer with a college professor and the two might not be able to exchange a single idea.

Architects, health care providers, insurance underwriters, plumbers, street pavers, street people, automotive servicers, kitchen workers, painters, musicians, movie makers, police officers (10-4)—all of these people have languages that are unique to their work.

How do impostors get away with their scams? They learn to talk the language of the field they wish to enter. Learning to talk the language is the first part of taking on a new job in a new field. The Ph.D. who takes a temporary job pumping gas or driving a taxi has to learn an entire new language. The taxi driver or gas pumper who takes a job parking cars at an elegant hotel has to learn an entire new language.

Words tell who we are, or pretend to be. They give us away as surely as our clothes do. Written words tell even more, for they reflect what is going on inside as well as outside the body. Words give away our geographic origins, our educational background, and our emotional outlook on life.

There used to be a man in show business who frequented the talk shows with his act—guessing where people came from just from having them talk for a few minutes. He could place an accent, listen to word clues and judge word pronunciation so well that he could often tell where a person was born, where they grew up and where they currently were living, just from the words.

Psychologists depend on words to uncover hidden meanings and repressed trauma in patients. The words flow from the feelings and provide clues to what's going on inside a person.

Believe it or not, you can tell a person's approximate age by listening to their word choices. Groovy, Right on, Hubba-hubba, I'm hip, I'm hep! For sure! Excellent!

IDIOMS

Using a language by following the rules often has strange results. The peculiarities of a language make it difficult for outsiders to learn. Try carrying on a conversation in another language after learning the functional phrases taught on language tapes.

To follow all the rules would be to overlook the special ways we talk to people. There's no way to define or explain idioms. They are the quirks of our language.

In writing, the overuse of these idioms can result in trite language. Not to use them results in stiff language. Consider carefully some of America's idioms:

It's me.
I like this *a lot.*
This isn't *much good.*
That's *pretty much* the same thing.
He's *mighty fond* of her.
Don't *bug* me.
I'm *used to* this way.
I didn't *used to be.*

I *take it* you want to marry me.
take great pains
get a head start
a stone's throw
on a roll
wing it

Idioms that are formed in combination with prepositions are called idiomatic prepositions and are discussed in Chapter 6.

SELECT WORDS CAREFULLY

Pay attention to meanings. Become intimately connected to your dictionary, thesaurus and any written material.

Read profusely. Notice how other writers use words. Try to get inside an author's mind and unlock the feelings and intentions of the writer as the writing was being done. It is very easy to read a paragraph, skim the words, and pull out a superficial meaning. But how much more rewarding it is when you can re-trace the thought process of the writer and determine what were the feelings at the moment the words were placed on paper (or into the computer)!

Select words carefully.

Know who you're writing to. Different messages require different words. The selection of words must fit the reader. What words would you choose to send a scathing memo to your boss, a make-nice memo to your staff, a request note to your spouse, an apologetic note to the principal, and a report to the board of directors.

Watch for unnecessary words. Read over what you have written and determine which words can be eliminated to keep your message succinct, yet flavorful. Look at the following phrases as examples of over-wordiness.

Wordy	*Succinct*
As per your request	As you requested
Until such time as	Until
We respectfully solicit	We ask
We are this day in receipt of	Today we received
In the event that	When/if
In regard to	Regarding
An invoice in the amount of $58	An invoice for $58
The foregoing	These
In reference to	Referring to

Under separate cover	Separately
Would you be so kind as to	Would you
For the duration of the year	For the year
At the present time	Presently
At your earliest convenience	Soon/promptly/immediately
Enclosed herewith is	Here is
At a later date	Later
To our mutual interest	Mutually
To spell out	To clarify
Due to the fact that	Because of
Mutually agreed upon time	At a time convenient to you
The above	This/these
Thanks and please advise	Please let us know

EXTRANEOUS WORDS

Look at the redundancy of some of the following words. Yet, these extra words pop up in much of today's correspondence.

Let's cooperate *together*.
I know you write stories, poems, articles, *and* etc.
Please meet a friend *of mine*.
The table was reserved *exclusively* for the big wigs.
The program continued *on* with unabated boredom.
They said that the work was produced on a *more* sounder basis.
In my opinion, *I think* she was wrong.
Each *and every* report was carefully recorded.
The speech was meant to get people off *of* their duffs.
It was the *general* consensus of opinion that it worked.
The audience rose *up* to speak shaking their fists.
The speaker responded *very* briefly.
The opponents had nothing in common *with each other*.
The whole encounter actually took only *about* five minutes.
We must *first* report this before we leave.
It happened about 7:30 P.M. *last night*.
We'll let you know *later* how it turned out.

THROWAWAY WORDS

What is worse than too many words is the use of the wrong words or the use of non-words. Every day, we hear the following, which have no reason for being:

Anyways/Anywheres	Toss the *s*. Anyway/Anywhere
Being that/Being as how	Since
Could of/Would of	Could have and would have.
Exsetera	Et cetera is pronounced like it's spelled. It means *and so forth*.
Enlargen	Enlarge
Enthused	The adjective is enthusiastic.
Had ought/Hadn't ought	One ought to or ought not to.
In regards to	If you are referencing, use *in regard to*.
Irregardless	No such word! (The prefix and suffix mean the same thing.)
Unmerciless	Ditto above.
Momento	This is Spanish. Do you mean memento, a souvenir?
Portentious	Portentous
Presumptious	Presumptuous is what you mean.
Prophesize	The verb is prophesy (sigh); the noun is prophecy (see).
Secondhanded	Toss away the *ed*.
Somewheres	Somewhere
Undoubtably	Undoubtedly incorrect!
Unequivocably	Unequivocally wrong!

EXERCISES
(Answers to exercises are in the Appendix.)

Make a list of technical words you had to learn to get along in your field of work.

Keep a notebook where you can list words you never heard before. Are they in the dictionary? or did someone make them up?

Make a collection of your own words (ones you make up to solve a deficiency).

Establish a check list to cover areas you need to monitor in your own writing. The list could include such things as: spelling, overuse of it, double verbs, extraneous words, verb/noun agreement, proper pronouns, overuse of commas, too many hyphens, or too many dashes or ellipses.

Try the exercises below.

1. For fun and profit (you'll gain a wealth of information about how words work) convert the words below into as many kinds of functions as you can. For instance: *Profit* is a noun. Change it into an adjective, verb, adverb, or anything else you can: profitable (adj.) profit (v.) profitize (v., why not?), profitably (adv.)

Not all the words are nouns. But they might be converted if you try.

discovery	generous	compare	beautifully
desire	lonely	describe	apparently
accident	similar	analyze	defiantly
grammar	humid	resent	ecstatically
miracle	efficient	confide	jokingly
apology	frivolous	exclude	apathetically

2. How many meanings can you devise for the following words (without consulting the dictionary).

light
down
up
round
run
dope
object
in
roll
well
commercial
mother
blood

3. Tighten up your writing. Take out the extra words below:
   a. Ken's acting was good enough to enable him to qualify for the leading role of a community theater.
   b. The play called for stage props of the family home type.
   c. Ken was told about three rules that should be observed.
   d. One was that sets which are damaged by the players are to be repaired.
   e. Another was that by the keeping of records, the repertory players could handle a variety of roles.

    f. In the period between September and December, Ken performed in four plays.

4. Reduce the following wordy sentences. Make them as concise as you can.

    a. Meanwhile, Barb took figure skating lessons and could be observed to be getting better each time.

    b. The company was involved in the task of reviewing the small print of her contract.

    c. The board members are of the opinion that her risk of injury is a detriment to the company.

    d. It is essential that steps be taken to remove her from this activity.

    e. Reference is made to the event three weeks ago in which she suffered a knee injury that kept her off of her feet for two days.

    f. The board should take the appropriate action to determine whether or not she should be allowed to continue.

    g. By acting now, we can decide this sooner than if we wait until a later date.

15

Structuring Sentences

The foundation of good writing is sentence structure. But how many people know how to structure simple sentences, compound sentences and complex sentences? And what difference does it make anyway? In this chapter, you'll learn how to write grownup sentences. You'll review clauses, phrases, parallel construction, misplaced modifiers and sentence overload. You'll also look into the pitfalls of double-verbing, a nasty habit that is perpetuated in much of today's business correspondence.

A sentence needs to be focused on a separate idea or on closely related ideas. It can take the form of a statement, a question, a command, a wish or an exclamation. A sentence can be very simple or very complex.

Take a simple subject, add a simple verb to tell what the subject is doing; add an object to tell us who or what is being done to; then throw in some phrases and a clause or two. Presto! You have a sentence.

But what if we need a phrase or clause to form the subject? Or a phrase or clause to define the verb? Now we're talking grammar!

This is a sentence:

Something is happening. (Subject—verb—complement)

This also is a sentence:

Something or other which I can't put my finger on is happening or about
to happen or did happen to me and others in my family who so far
have forgotten to tell me about the event which I probably will find
out about in due time or at the time when it is my turn to know about
such things.

Would anyone in the class like to parse this one? Parse, dissect, diagram, explain, or describe the component parts? Come back to this after you finish this chapter and try it again.

The following paragraphs are samples of several different ways of writing, from the simple to the verbose. They depict various styles of writing and degrees of complexity. Look them over carefully to determine how each has its place and each has its own style.

SIMPLE WRITING

A house is for sale. The house belongs to the Morgans. The Morgans are a family of four. The house has three bedrooms. It has two bathrooms. The house also contains a living room, dining room and kitchen. A basement is finished for use. The lawn needs work. A garage will hold two cars. It is attached to the house.

GROWNUP WRITING

The house belonging to the Morgans, a family of four, is for sale. The house, which contains three large bedrooms and two bathrooms, also has a spacious living room, a dining room that will hold large family dinners, and a well-equipped yellow and white kitchen. In addition, the basement, finished with extra rooms, and the lawn, which needs some work, are added assets to this fine house. Still more: a two-car garage is attached to the house.

SHORT WRITING

The Morgan house, containing three bedrooms and two baths, living and dining rooms, kitchen and finished basement, is for sale. A two-car garage is attached to the house. The lawn needs work.

EVEN SHORTER

For sale by family of four: 3 br/2 bath, lr, dr, kitchen, finished basement, 2-car garage.

PRETENTIOUS, VERBOSE, FLOWERY WRITING

The Morgan family, a respected family of four—mother, father and two lovely children—is selling their beautiful home. Three large, friendly bedrooms and two full baths have provided a wonderful living space for the family; they are heartsick about having to sell it.

The wide open living room is lighted naturally by two elegant picture windows that invite the afternoon sun. The ambience of the large family dining room awaits the holiday banquet as easily as it encourages simple family meals. Adjacent, the early sun floods the yellow and white kitchen with delightful effect on morning coffee.

Below, a fully-finished basement begs for attention: a den, office space, private hobby room, and recreation room. As if this weren't enough, a garage, big enough to hold two family autos, is attached to the side of the house, keeping occupants dry in rainy weather. No dash to the door for the lucky family that purchases this house.

All of this magic—grownup writing, parallel writing, understandable, idea-producing, explanatory writing—is obtained by using all three kinds of sentences: simple, compound and complex (or a combination of any of them). Just what is a sentence? How can we put one together?

Simple Sentence

The idea of a simple sentence is to include one subject and one predicate. Does anyone know what a predicate is? Okay, then let's call it the subject and the rest of the sentence.

A simple sentence contains the subject and the rest of the sentence. The rest of the sentence contains a verb. (A verb makes this sentence a clause, an independent clause. It stands on its own.) The sentence could have several phrases (the additions without the extra verb), but in the end it comprises only one independent clause. All of the following are simple sentences.

The company held a picnic.

The ABC Company *with all its six branches* held a picnic *in the park*. (The emphasized portions are prepositional phrases.)

The ABC Company, its employees and officers, held a picnic and family outing in the park. (Compound subject and multiple objects, but only one verb.)

The company held a family outing and presented the annual report during a picnic in the park on Saturday. (Compound verbs and objects, additional prepositional phrases: *during a picnic*, *in the park*, *on Saturday*, but only one subject.)

The prime requisite of a simple sentence is that it has only one independent clause and no dependent set of words (clause) containing a verb of its own.

A simple sentence may use an action verb or a stop-action verb. The action verb requires a direct object (and perhaps an indirect object).

The stop-action verb may be followed by an adjective (that describes the subject), a compliment (that completes or repeats the subject), or an adverb that describes the verb. A stop-action verb does not have an object.

The company held its picnic for 300 employees. (Action verb is *held*; direct object is *picnic*; and indirect object is *300 employees.*)

The day was warm. (Stop-action verb, and adjective *warm* describes *day.*)

The day was Saturday. (Stop-action verb, and *Saturday* complements and repeats *day.*)

All those people were served easily. (Stop-action verb *were served*; adverb *easily* describes how.)

COMPOUND SENTENCE

A compound sentence is simply a connection of two simple sentences (two independent clauses). They can be joined in four ways: 1) a comma followed by a conjunction, 2) a semicolon, or 3) a semicolon followed by a conjunction. 4) A very short compound sentence may be connected with only the conjunction.

Two simple sentences: The food was the best part of the picnic. Every department contributed some of the food.

1) The hotdogs and beans were furnished by the Accounting Department, and the hamburgers and chips were brought by the Advertising Department.
2) The salads were made by members of Shipping; the bread and rolls came from Purchasing.
3) The beverages were supplied by Management; and the beer was a gift from the chief executives.
4) The pies came from Sales and the cake was baked by the receptionist.

COMPLEX SENTENCES

To form a complex sentence, simply add a clause—the phrase that includes a verb. We reviewed them in Chapters 4, 5, and 7. A complex sentence contains one dependent clause (the main simple sentence) and one or more dependent clauses (they need the sentence to exist).

A clause adds information about a subject, object or verb and is joined to the simple sentence by a conjunction. That's all. Not as complex as it sounds, is it?

The following are complex sentences. We took the four examples above and supplied a verb and additional information to produce clauses.

1) The hotdogs and beans were furnished by the Accounting Department, who *did* all the cooking themselves. (Adjective clause modifying Accounting Department.)

2) The salads, which *were made* by members of Shipping, tasted fresh and appetizing. (Adjective clause modifying salads.)

3) Although we *didn't expect* it, the beverages were supplied by Management. (Adverb clause modifying were supplied.)

4) Pies were the dessert *furnished* by Sales. (Noun clause complementing the subject.)

5) The contribution *made* by the receptionist was the cake. (Noun clause replacing the subject.)

The last two examples, noun clauses, are on the borderline of the complex sentence. They are included here to show how close they come to the border. Technically, a clause includes a verb. When the subject clause fits that requirement, it becomes a contributor to a complex sentence.

If we omitted the verb in the clause, the sentences would be simple sentences:

4) Pies were the dessert from Sales.

5) The contribution of the receptionist was the cake.

A cause and effect sentence shows that something happens as a result of something else. Try using a complex sentence (with a clause) instead of a compound sentence with an inappropriate connector. Replace the compound sentence replaced by the awkward *so* or *but* with a reversed sentence that begins with a clause.

Avoid:

The speaker noted the hour was early, so he continued taking questions.
Everyone in the audience was tired, so they applauded and got up to leave.
The orchestra hadn't rehearsed but they played well.

Reversed:

Noting the hour was early, the speaker continued taking questions.

Because everyone in the audience was tired, they applauded and got up
to leave.

Although they hadn't rehearsed, the orchestra played well.

COMPOUND COMPLEX SENTENCES

Check the requirements for both the compound and complex sentences.
Compound sentences require two independent clauses (two simple sentences); complex sentences require a dependent clause or two. Put them
together, just like in science or math, for the finished product.

If you want to take over the company, you need at least $5 million;
clearly, a small down payment and a promise might get the paper
work started.

The Board of Directors heard about the takeover, but failing to act
immediately, they lost the advantage.

Mergers and takeovers cause problems over and above what occurs
daily; yet, the emerging company always comes out stronger.

CLAUSES, PHRASES

Clauses and phrases make simple writing more grownup. Variety is the
element that identifies grownup writing. If we wrote in simple sentences
all the time, life would get boring. This is what clauses and phrases are for,
to spice up the writing, make it interesting, understandable, and clear.

PARALLEL IDEAS

Take an idea, identify what you are talking about (subject), choose the
verb that best tells what is going on, and the object that receives the action.
Carefully select the phrases and clauses that modify and connect these
ideas. When you connect ideas, make sure you choose the same kinds of
words in the parts being connected.

Making sure that the parts are the same is as important as fitting the
right pieces of pipe together in plumbing. If the parts are from different
manufacturers or made of different materials, there may be an interruption
of flow.

The idea supported the plan and is an identification of the project.

Use either:

The idea supported the plan and identified the project.
Or:
The idea supports the plan and is an identification of the project.

Keep the tense of verbs equal, in the same time zone. Be sure that both belong in the same time zone! If you discover that one part belongs in another time zone, sometimes it is best to give it a separate sentence.

I visited San Francisco and found it *was* a beautiful city.

Actually, San Francisco still *is* a beautiful city. That *was* should be *is*. This appears to defy the parallelism in order to maintain honesty, but it doesn't. Look at the active verbs. The *is* lies in the clause that is the object of *found*.

I visited San Francisco and found it is a beautiful city.

The *visited* and *found* maintain the past tense in fine parallel form.
A huge problem in parallel writing arises when we use a series. Sometimes we get lost before we come to the end.

My decision was to ride the trolley, visit the museums, drive across the bridge, shop at the big department stores, and spending the rest of the day on the wharf.

Whoops! The verbs are: ride, visit, drive, shop and spending. One of them doesn't belong. Can you tell which one? Of course you can. Yet, grownups put together series like this in much of their writing. It's the way we think. Knowing this, it shouldn't be too difficult to watch out for mismatched parts of a series.

If you're hungry you can enjoy a snack of cheese and crackers, sipping on a milkshake, indulging in a yogurt sundae, or pick a few tomatos from the garden.
Verbs: enjoy, sipping, indulging, and pick. Choose verbs either with or without the *ing* and proceed.

The very ridiculous happens when we mismatch ideas. That is, we combine two separate ideas in a sentence. Remember, a sentence needs to be focused on a single idea.

> The picnic began with a rain shower that dampened the mood, and continued when the company president arrived to make a speech.

This item, if it appeared in a company newsletter, could cause trouble for the writer. Did the rain continue or did the picnic continue with a damp mood? Separate the two events to make clear the mood didn't have anything to do with the president.

> The picnic began with a rain shower that dampened the mood. The rain continued as the company president arrived to make a speech.

Or:

> The picnic began with a rain shower that dampened the mood. The picnic continued (even picked up) as the company president arrived to make a speech.

Whew! That's better. It could save somebody's job.

CLOSELY RELATED IDEAS

Sentences must be checked just like computer disks to be sure some kind of strange virus hasn't invaded. Sometimes thoughts race during the writing process, resulting in sentences that contain diverse information.

> The files are in a bad mess, and the receptionist is home sick with a cold.
> Three people from the front office are out sick and the telephones are ringing.

The above two sentences are somewhat related in the writer's mind, but not in the sentences. Relate them by supplying information in appropriate clauses:

> The files are in a bad mess because the receptionist who normally handles this duty is home sick with a cold.
> Since three people from the front office are out sick, the telephones are ringing with no one to answer them.

Too Much! Overload!

The following paragraph contains one single sentence!

> Occasionally, when we're in a hurry, we write too much in one sentence, cluttering it up with detail that should be relegated to additional sentences, which would place close ideas together and leave the other ideas for sentences by themselves, sentences that would read more easily because of the shorter format and the fewer details within a single sentence, causing readers to be able to extract the idea being communicated with less trouble than a sentence such as this causes a reader.

Pant, pant! Pity the reader who has to wade through a sentence like this. Keep yours shorter. Leave out repetition, simplify sentences, modify what is necessary and scrap the rest.

Over-writing is simply unclear thinking. Get your act together and decide exactly what you want to say before starting to write.

Double Verbs, Modifiers, Nouns

So many communicators have only a shadowy idea of what they want to say. Grasping for the right verb, they often supply choices for the recipient of the message. This is understandable in spoken language, acceptable to a point.

However, in written communications, there is little excuse for double verbing, that is, grasping for the right verb.

A favorite example of double verbing:

> I thought I would like to try to sit down to attempt to make up or produce a memo to you to start to explain the altercation yesterday.

Count the verbs: thought, would like, try, sit down, attempt, make up, produce, start, explain! Too many! Choose two, even three, but no more.

I'm attempting to produce a memo to explain the altercation yesterday. Look over something you have written lately and pick out the double (or triple or more) verbs. Could they have been cut back. In much writing today, the message sender gives the message recipient choices.

I want to *extend or direct* my apologies to you.
Let's meet to *plan and outline* the report.
Over lunch we can *discuss and talk about* the new recruit.

In each of the above sentences, the reader has to make the choice that should have been made by the writer. More direct sentences occur when the writer determines exactly what is being said.

I want to direct my apologies to you.
Let's meet to outline the report.
Over lunch we can discuss the new recruit.

Double adjectives and adverbs suffer the same malaise. By putting thoughts down quickly, a writer doesn't take time to sort and choose. They may end up with sentences like the following:

She was *pleased and happy* to note the appointment.
When she sat down, she appeared *relaxed and contented*.
He admitted he felt *lonely and left out* when the group met.
After the *tall and rangy* man entered the room, it quieted down.

The emphasized words in each sentence are repetitious. They say nearly the same thing. By using more words than you need, you are asking the reader to choose the appropriate word. Don't relinquish your authority as the writer. Know that sentences appear much stronger when that choice is made in the writing:

She was pleased to note the appointment.
When she sat down, she appeared contented.
He admitted he felt lonely when the group met.
After the rangy man entered the room, it quieted down.

Some writers even try to leave the subject up to the reader.

Twenty *boys or youngsters* showed up for practice.
The *limbs and the twigs* of the trees had been blown down in the storm.
The playing court was filled with cracked *cement and concrete*.
The practice *workouts and exercises* left the kids tired.

Sloppy writing occurs with unclear thinking and scant editing. Write down your message with all the choices on the first draft. When you're finished, go back and scope the *ands* to eliminate redundant words and ideas. The way you edit is an important part of your unique style.

MISPLACED MODIFIERS

Some of the world's best jokes come out of misplaced modifiers. When those pesky little things end up in the wrong place, we get sentences like:

We need a tool for fastening a mirror that is made with a small motor.
The clerk handed me the motor and turned to another customer carelessly.
The new instrument in my hand represented greater repair of our home with its red, shiny blades.
You only say it costs $14.98?

Modifiers must be placed close to the words they modify. Rewrite the above and move the modifiers where they belong:

We need a tool *that is made with a small motor* for fastening a mirror.
The clerk *carelessly* handed me the motor and turned to another customer.
The new instrument *with its red, shiny blades* in my hand, represented greater repair of our home.
You say it costs *only* $14.98?

"If I've said it once, I've said it a thousand times," began Miss Miller. "Always put the modifier next to the word it modifies."

EXERCISES
(Answers to exercises are in the Appendix.)

1. Combine the following information into one simple sentence. Now write the information into a compound sentence. And try a complex sentence.

   The corner deli was held up last night. The clerk was alone in the store. The robber took all the money.

2. Try another:
   The Department of Fisheries issued a new regulation. The department is directed by Joe Bird. The regulation is harsh.

3. Move the modifiers to make sense:
   a. The restaurant was cited for cleanliness in a tough part of town.
   b. Most people on leave of absence offer too many excuses who don't want to work.
   c. Approaching the soup kitchen, a long line of people is visible from the south.
   d. We intended to spend all day in the kitchen which holds 50 people working and helping out.
   e. By the end of the day, the food went to all the street people that we had cooked.

4. Rewrite the following sentences for more clarity. Watch the parallel structure, verb use, misplaced modifiers, and confusing sentence type.
   a. The firefighter didn't carry a hatchet which was dangerous.
   b. Three windows were broken in the fire and two people find themselves carried down the ladders.
   c. All the residents escaped injury except the tired firefighter who was overcome by smoke.
   d. A fire like this can only start in the stairwell.
   e. Out of the ashes will rise a new building which is still smoldering.

5. Remove the extra verbs below:
   a. Ken and Barb began to realize they felt their lives were not useful.
   b. They knew they could read in the paper what they believed to be the reality of the world around them.
   c. They thought they might be able to try to do something useful with their time away from work.
   d. Could they be useful if they registered to take classes to learn to be socially responsible?
   e. Both of them resolved to take a look at what the options would be if they decided to expand their horizons.

16

Building Paragraphs

With a solid sentence foundation, paragraph building becomes a cinch. Do you remember the topic sentence of Miss Miller's classes? Do you remember how it can head up the paragraph, end it, or lie buried in the middle of it? In this chapter you'll look at topic sentences and how they form paragraphs as mini-stories and you'll look at paragraphs as one-liners. You'll even look at ways to transport from one to another.

Putting paragraphs together is more like playing with blocks than you may realize. Each paragraph is a module of its own which must be made to fit smoothly into the format of the entire piece of writing.

A paragraph can be complete with a very few words, a single sentence, or a series of sentences. Effective writing throws in a bit of each to produce a variety of paragraph lengths. Repetitious paragraph lengths work much like a sleeping potion, especially in business writing.

A professional writer tells how she discovered the deadly repetition of paragraph lengths when she switched to a word processor. For the first time, she saw her writing as a pattern on the screen and was horrified to realize she habitually wrote four-line paragraphs. To avoid this pitfall, pick up a random piece of writing from your desk and turn it upside down. Do the paragraphs all look the same? If so, vary them; make some longer, some shorter.

A short paragraph grabs attention.

A longer paragraph draws that attention out, telling the reader there is much to be learned about this particular idea. That's one of the reasons for having a long paragraph. Another reason is to provide a canvas for a complete message, one that may be reduced or diluted if it were split up into several short paragraphs. The long paragraph definitely has its place in business writing.

Review the last two paragraphs. Notice the differences, the similarities.

TOPIC SENTENCES

Surely, you recall Miss Miller teaching topic sentences. That was the day you first were exposed to the subject of paragraph construction. Perhaps you have since learned to construct paragraphs subconsciously—many get through long writing careers unaware of how they do it. If you are aware, subconsciously or not, that paragraphs have a form, your writing may utilize it without much thought. If you are not aware of this form, let's review. We can take what Miss Miller taught you, and expand it to fit your needs now, as a grownup.

A topic sentence sets the tone and subject of a paragraph. It may be placed up front, at the end, or in the middle. Everything in that paragraph must define, expand upon, compare to or contradict that statement. A topic sentence can be stated more than once in more than one way.

Red

Red is a color close to my heart. Actually, it is the color of my heart, and blood vessels, and much of my body. Red is the color that means life and beauty, much like the pulsing of the vital organs, the throbbing of a heart. Because red is such a color of health and life, it is often referred to as a vibrant color—vibrant meaning full of life. *Yes, red is a vibrant color, as close as my heart.*

The above paragraph carries the topic sentence throughout (red is the color), but the more definitive sentence is repeated at the beginning and end. A paragraph that follows on the subject of red might contain a topic sentence about the color red as found in nature, or in literature, or in music. Or it could describe the way a particular painter used the color red, or didn't use it. Can you see the flexibility, the space to move around with your topic sentence? The topic sentences in the following paragraphs are underlined.

Red is a color found in nature. Because it is bright, red is a favorite color of fruits and flowers, such as cherries, apples, raspberries, roses, hibiscus and rhododendrons. Tomatos and red peppers seem to be the only red vegetables, unless you count red cabbage and red celery. Animals too reflect the red color, as in red-tailed deer, red squirrel and red fox. The red coloring found in birds is also distinctive, usually found in males.

Because emotions are strong, they elicit strong reactions. Anger, jealousy, rage are among the strongest. Sexual desire is also considered a strong psychological reaction in humans. These strong emotions can be enhanced with the use of color. *Red is the color most often connected with strong emotions.*

When discussing red, the human body must be included. Red is found in skin tones, hair coloring, and in a person's shy blush. Red is the color of the blood and most internal organs. We even refer to some people as rednecks when they spout biased ideas. *The human body contains many references to red, even artificially.* Coloring is added to many human bodies in the form of red nail polish, lipstick and rouge. Even some eye makeup is colored red. *Red is a significant color when attached to the human body.*

TRANSITION WORDS

In the construction of paragraphs, it is also necessary to link them somehow. That is, it is necessary to provide transition words that tie the ideas of the paragraphs together.

A few techniques that may help:

Use words that automatically give direction to writing by setting the time or space of the topic, such words as: yet, still, next, first, finally, however, moreover, thus.

Use a pronoun in a paragraph opening sentence that refers to a noun in the previous paragraph.

> The catalog that comes with each machine tells everything about the fully automatic Multi-key Typewriter. A primary accessory is the error eraser.
> *Another of its* accessories is the adjustable set of keys.

Pick up a word from the previous paragraph and use it early in the following paragraph.

> You'll especially like the ease with which the automatic keyboard fits your fingertips.
> *This ease* will be reflected in the comfort you feel during the work day and the extra energy you'll enjoy after working long hours.

Parallel construction is another technique for tying paragraphs together. Begin each paragraph with a similar sentence; then go on to fill out the paragraph to follow that topic.

> Red is a wild color.
> Red is a hot color.

Red is a sexy color.
Red is a warning color.
Red is a color with many intensities.

Read through a piece of business writing, a newspaper item, a magazine article, and watch for the transition techniques. Become aware of how they are used by good writers. You won't have to make a conscious effort to build your paragraphs; by knowing how, the construction will fall into place easily.

COMPUTERIZED WRITING

Using the word processor to create pieces of writing is a snap when you utilize a simple system for outlining. After you have brainstormed and set down a number of ideas that you wish to include in your piece, write them all down in a list on the word processor.

Brainstorming

Brainstorming is a problem-solving technique used in groups to produce ideas. One person is designated to write down everything said. The others come up with creative suggestions which are written down without judgment. It's a spontaneous, no-holds-barred way of stimulating original thought.

Individuals can brainstorm in similar ways, writing down all the ideas they can drum up, without passing judgment on thoughts that present themselves. A quiet room and a yellow pad work for some. Others prefer a recording machine. Many writers use their word processors, darkening the screen or covering it up to free the brain to take off in flights of fancy and originality.

In a brainstorming session, the subject red turned up a page full of ideas. They seemed to fall into several areas of interest about the color, listed below:

Chromatic Hue
In Nature
Emotional Color
Political Connotations
The Human Body
Danger
Shades of Red
Red Words

Take this list, rearrange the ideas in whatever order that seems to work, and you have the outline for an essay on the color red. You can make that essay as short as a sentence:

> The color red, the brightest of the colors, is found abundantly in nature, is an emotional color with political connotations, is a primary color of the human body, is used to signify danger, comes in many shades and shows up in such word messages as redneck and red hot.

By completing each thought with a full sentence, you may construct a longer paragraph. Get carried away and write several paragraphs about each thought on the list, you'll achieve a full essay. When you get really steamed up, you may want to try writing an entire chapter about each topic. That's how books are planned and written. The best writers use this technique.

Use the computer with its marvelous ways of expanding and its ability to move ideas around. Not only will you find more fun in putting down ideas, but you'll find them easier to edit.

Hint: After many years writing professionally, a friend suggested that the best place to find that important opening paragraph is at the end of your work. For some reason, the human mind likes to save the best part until last. Look at your final paragraph and decide whether or not to move it to the front.

EXERCISE

Brain-storm a color of your choice: blue, green, yellow, orange, violet, black, white, brown, silver, gold, puce, turquoise or chartreuse. Write down everything you can think of in connection with that color. Don't worry about form. Write down ideas all over the paper. After you have exhausted all your ideas, look over what you have jotted down. You'll find some similar things; draw lines around them, or mark them with colored pencil. Make a list of all these groups. (Miss Miller delighted in calling them sets.) Using this outline, write an essay or a poem—or a book.

Only after you have written out all your ideas, go back and edit. Find your topic sentences. Look at transition words. Read your essay outloud and listen to its rhythm. Do you find your lead paragraph at the end or at the beginning where it belongs?

Four Guides to Better Spelling

The most attention in grammar seems to be aimed at spelling. If all the words are spelled right, we feel we've done a good job. Of course that isn't quite true, but the emphasis on spelling is extremely important. The first notion that must be erased from most bad spellers' minds is that they are bad spellers. The four ways to improve spelling are the Root Word Approach, the Prefix/Suffix Approach, the Sounding Approach (attention to correct pronunciation), and the Look-It-Up-and-Memorize-It Approach. Miss Miller's Rules are included (in case you forgot them). Spelling is a visual skill. You need to pay attention with all of the senses and implant the word into your visual memory forever, as securely as spelling your own name.

Recently a proud banner went up in a neighborhood shopping plaza announcing: Florist Comeing Soon! Two weeks passed before someone whited out the *e* to correct the spelling. Readerboards notoriously contain misspelled words. Of late, they're even showing up on television news shows!

Mention spelling (sometimes grammar will do it) and you hear, "Oh, poor me! I can't spell worth a darn. I've always been a bad speller."

With that attitude, you'll always be a bad speller.

The secret to becoming a good speller is simple: pay attention. Read and become familiar with words, lots of them, even if you don't always know what they mean. Become aware of how words are put together with suffixes and prefixes (endings and beginnings). Discover the world of root words, the places where words come from. The American language combines languages from cultures around the world; it's no wonder that spelling is a challenge. Some word people (lexicologists) estimate the language contains contributions from more than 50 countries.

The four methods presented here are offered as helpers to anyone wanting to improve spelling techniques. No single method will work in all situations, but you may be surprised how often you will employ one or more of the methods.

THE ROOT WORD APPROACH

You've noticed how often many words will stem from approximately the same word. For instance: medical, medication, medicine, medicinal; hypnosis, hypnotize, hypnotic, hypnotical; tense, tension, tenseness, tensity, pretension, extension.

The root word approach suggests that you find another related word that you do know how to spell and apply similar spelling to the word you're looking for.

If you wondered how to spell medic—nal (is it medicanal, medicenal, medicunal?), you might look at medicine (which you are sure of) and apply the same spelling (choosing the *i*).

When you know that the *sci* in science is carried over into words like conscious and conscience, you won't have trouble with them anymore.

Do you spell preten—ion and exten—ion with *s* or *t*? Can you spell tension? Sure you can. Spell the others the same way, with the *s*.

THE PREFIX/SUFFIX METHOD

This system also requires some sense of root words. It also employs a mathematical formula that's as simple as adding $1 + 1 = 2$.

If a prefix ends in the same letter that the root word begins, add them together and get two letters. (*un-necessary, ac-commodate, im-mediate, il-legitimate, in-novation*). If the prefix ends in a letter other than the beginning of the root word, there is no doubling: recommend, disappear, resistant, acoustics, renovation, ineligible.

The same mathematical formula works for suffixes: commonness, humanness, certainness, logically, finally, grandness, civilness, probably, grandly.

THE SOUNDING METHOD

Here's the one Miss Miller taught for a few semesters. "Sound it out," you recall her saying patiently. The sound-it-out method is called *phonetics*.

The catch is that many of us come from parts of the country that speak with different sounds. So it is logical for people to misspell words the way they missound them.

Public schools seem to favor the phonetic system of teaching words and spelling on an intermittent basis. Some of us grew up learning the phonetic system; others grew up during a period that educators were discounting it. Much can be said both in favor of and against phonetic spelling. Many of our words can be sounded out and spelled accurately using the smattering of spelling guides. However, you'll recall that you probably learned the word *exception* in connection with spelling rules. There seem to be more exceptions than there are rules.

How do you teach the different spellings for paired words such as: pair/pear, bear/bare; fair/fare? In some parts of the country, the following words may sound alike: fear, fare, for, fair, far, and give spelling teachers the willies. Try tear, tar, tire in the Deep South.

We had a President who probably could never spell *government* because he pronounced it with a *b* (gubment). We had another President who pronounced *nuclear* with an extra *u* (nucular). When we pronounce words wrong, the probability of spelling them correctly decreases. Refer to dictionaries for help.

Realtors themselves seem to have trouble pronouncing the word correctly: real-tors and not real-a-tors. And athletes like to add an extra syllable in their name too: ath-a-letes. If you can't pronounce it right, you will have trouble spelling it right.

The big debate continues nationwide as to the pronunciation of harassment. (However, there need be no doubt the word contains two *s*'s.) Not exactly a scientific observation, but it seems men prefer the accent on the second syllable; women and British people prefer the first.

Sound out the following words and watch out for the sneaky letters that seem not to belong there: length, strength, height, perform, surprise, prescription, recognize, hindrance (only 2 syllables), athletics (only 3 syllables), library, government, congratulations. (How often have you seen a congratulations sign on a high school readerboard spelled with a *d*?)

THE LOOK-IT-UP-AND-MEMORIZE-IT METHOD

The most useful way to become a good speller is to carry a dictionary with you and look up words you're unsure of. But promise yourself to look up a word only once. Then give yourself a system for remembering.

Aberration contains an *aber* and a *ration*.
Apparition has an *ap* prefix with a *parition* root.
Accommodation duplicates ²/₅ of its consonants.
Pursue is what you do when you see a purse you want.

Iridescent descends (nearly) from the iris.

Privilege stands on a leg and not on a ledge.

Contemptuous is a relationship (*con*) that tempts *u* and *ous*.

Personal is just for one (*n*); personnel is for more (add the *nel* suffix).

Aqua and all its watery derivatives are the only words that begin with *aq*. The other similar-sounding words need the *c* insert: acquire, acquaint, acquit.

The only *ceed* words are proceed, exceed and succeed. All the others are *cede* words: accede, intercede, precede, etc. The lone exception is supersede which sounds like one of this family but isn't!

Certain words in your vocabulary probably have bothered you for years. Decide to look them up one last time. Make a rhyme or jingle to help you remember them (the naughtier the jingle, the easier you'll remember). Keep your dictionary close until you discover one day that you refer to it less and enjoy spelling more.

Here's one way to build memory: There is no *e* on the end of develop, but there is on the end of an envelope (noun). The verb envelop lacks the *e*. Use this poem:

Devel op is enough to see (You don't need an optometrist.)
It doesn't have to end in *e*.
Envelope may go express
An antelope is hard to dress.

If no one else understands your jingles, don't mind. If jingles help you remember how words are spelled, only you have to understand them.

Miss Miller's Rules

I before *E*

The more people try to develop rules for spelling, the more mixed up we become. It seems that there are more exceptions to these rules than there are standard uses for them. However, a few ideas may serve as guidelines to improve spelling.

I before *e* except after *c*
or when sounded like *a*
as in neighbor and weigh.

Just as quickly as you learned that rule, you began to unravel the numbers of exceptions.

Seize the weird counterfeit heights with a sleight of hand.

Memorize that sentence and you'll know most of the exceptions.

Ending in *Y*

When a word ends in *y*, there are two rules. If the *y* has a consonant before it, change the *y* to *i* before adding a suffix except *ing*: (accompany, accompanies; worry, worries, worried; marry, marries, married). But: accompanying, worrying, marrying.

If the *y* follows a vowel, the second rule says, simply add the suffix: monkeying, monkeyed, journeying, journeyed.

One twist to the rule is its opposite: if a word ends in *ie* you change the *ie* to *y* before adding the suffix *ing*. Belying (belie), dying (die), vying (vie), lying (lie), tying (tie).

Ending in *O*

Sometimes it seems that spelling specialists make up rules to fill up their notebooks. While many are important to retain a kind of lexical history of words and some are useful to aid in pronunciation, a few of the rules just don't make sense. Four of these rules concern the plural forms of nouns ending in *o*.

Miss Miller's four rules:

1) Add an *s* to words ending with *o* preceded by a vowel: radio, studio, video, portfolio.
2) Add an *s* to musical terms ending in *o*: solo, piano, fortissimo, soprano, mezzo, crescendo, banjo.
3) Add *es* to certain nouns ending in *o* preceded by a consonant: tomato, potato, veto, hero, tuxedo, dynamo, tornado, torpedo. (Other nouns ending in *o* take the simple *s*.)
4) Make your own choice with other words ending in *o*. You may choose either the *s* or the *es*: motto, zero, cargo, memento, volcano.

A reasonable person can easily see there is no significance in adding *s* to some nouns and *es* to others. There is no spelling, national origin or word meaning similarities (except the musical terms).

Wouldn't it be simpler—and more reasonable—to condense these four rules into one? When making plurals of nouns ending in *o*, add *s*.

The following words are perfectly clear: tomatos, potatos, vetos, heros, tuxedos, dynamos, tornados, torpedos, mottos, zeros, cargos, mementos, volcanos.

Short vowels

When adding a suffix (*ed, ing, er*) to a word ending in a short vowel (the one that doesn't say its own name) and a single consonant, double the consonant to retain the short sound to the preceding vowel.

hop/hopping/hopped

Long vowels

When doing the same with a word ending in *e* preceded by a single consonant, drop the *e* and add the suffix, thus retaining the long vowel sound: hope (hoping, hoped), desire (desiring, desirable, desirous), spike (spiking, spiked), excuse (excusing, excusable).

Words that sound a long vowel usually end with an *e*, which provides the clue when to remove the *e* and add *ing*. A word like *come* that nearly says its own name doesn't call for the doubling of letters. (coming, comer)

Consonant-vowel-consonant

When a one-syllable word ends with a consonant-vowel-consonant combination, double the final consonant before adding a suffix that begins with a vowel: tan (tanning, tanner, tannest), tar (tarred, tarring), big (bigger, biggest), run (running, runner).

When a two-syllable word ends with the consonant-vowel-consonant combination, the same rule applies *if* the word is pronounced with an accent on the second syllable. (Refer, confer, occur, allot, begin) Refer (referring, referral, referred), confer (conferred, conferring), occur (occurred, occurring), allot (allotting, allotted), begin (beginning).

When the suffix you wish to add to these words does not begin with a vowel, you simply add the suffix: conferment, allotment, movement. (Some notable exceptions are: judgment, argument, acknowledgment. The English retain the *e* in judgement, acknowledgement.)

A NOTE FOR NORTHERN AMERICANS

The closer you get to the Canadian border, the more opportunities you have for lousing up your spelling. You see, Canadians are related to the British who have their own way of spelling. They get the *s* and the *z* mixed up sometimes. They also use the *u* more often than we do. And they leave the *e* in places we have removed it.

Typical British (Canadian) spelling: honour, colour, favour, theatre, centre, judgement, acknowledgement.

SPELLING SIMPLIFIED

Since words began to be printed on paper, people have been trying to simplify spelling. George Bernard Shaw was among many learned people to suggest simplified spelling. Many attempts have followed, particularly in the United States where the language is made up of many other languages.

When Theodore Roosevelt was President, at the beginning of this century, he sought to simplify the language by accepting a list of about 300 words prepared by a special panel called the Simplified Spelling Board. He asked federal employees to adopt the new spelling for such words as: *tho* for *though*, *thru* for *through*, *laf* for *laugh*, *bot* for *bought*, *donut* for *doughnut*, *enuf* for *enough*. The ensuing ruckus from Congress and the nation's newspapers caused President Roosevelt to re-think and rescind his order.

Many word endings that have been cluttered up with extra letters are now disappearing. Once spelled cigarette, the word has become cigaret. Others are the *gue* words, such as dialogue, monologue, and catalogue. These now can be spelled acceptably as dialog, monolog, catalog. The *ue* was retained from the French to make sure we used the hard *g* sound. Little question remains that the extra letters have served their purpose.

Don't dismay at this wonderful language of ours as did President Andrew Jackson when he cried out in frustration, "It's a damn poor mind that can think of only one way to spell a word."

EXERCISE

Keep a dictionary of your choice close at hand during the next few weeks. Refer to it as often as you need—to check words and correct them if necessary. Try using the methods discussed here; become aware of clues to spelling. Tune in to the sound of words.

18

Numbers

Since many business people work with numbers, the subject deserves its own chapter. Confusion exists as to whether or not to use numbers as words, when to use them as figures, and how to write them. Here you'll review using numbers in dates, money, inventory, temperature, fractions and percentage, dimensions, weights and measures, and addresses. You'll also delve into the mystifying meanings and uses of cardinals and ordinals.

NUMBERS (WHEN TO WRITE THEM OUT)

Numbers are used often in business writing, from an invoice to an annual report, and in personal writing, from baby's weight to the settlements in wills. Not much attention is paid to these numbers until they appear in courts of law or collection notices.

Generally, numbers from one through ten are written out. Numbers 11 and above are written in figures, numerals.

The city has four hospitals and 490 physicians.

The 23 nurses at one hospital comprise less than five percent of the staff.

The exceptions make up this chapter and include much that Miss Miller never even thought about.

One guideline suggests that when you are using a group of numbers in a particular context, either use all numerals or all words. The decision which to use depends on the majority of the numbers. If most of your numbers are under ten, write out the one or two that are over. If most of the numbers are above 11, use numerals for the few that are under.

The package contained two scissors, four rolls of tape, six bandages and thirty aspirins. Bandages come in separate packages of 500, 250, 50, 30 and 6.

Incidentally, Miss Miller used to abhor the use of *over* when talking about numbers. She preferred *above* or *more than*. However, most number users sprinkle their work with phrases like over 40, over $3 million, over two dollars. The way of the user seems to over-rule Miss Miller on this one. You decide which you prefer.

Business related injuries number over 3,000 a year and cost over $150,000.
Business related injuries number above 3,000 a year and cost more than $150,000.

Too often, the effect of a business report is lost to the cumbersome, monotonous recital of numbers, too long and too detailed to be under- standable. This is the time to find an easier-to-read version by choosing indefinite words when summarizing the numbers and spell them out:

Thousands of dollars were lost because of bad planning.
Letters numbered in the hundreds.
People in their twenties exude hope for recovery.
Give me a half minute to think.

Miss Miller cautioned us about beginning a sentence with a numeral. You may want to avoid beginning a sentence with a number of any kind. When it is absolutely, positively, no-other-way-to-do-it unavoidable to begin a sentence with a number, write it out, however cumbersome it may be. Most times, however, it is possible to re-cast the sentence to move the number inside.

2,314 responses came from angry constituents. (no)
Responses from 2,314 angry constituents were received.
Twenty-eight people attended the open hearing. (no)
The open hearing was attended by 28 people.

The dilemma of writing two numbers back-to-back when they could be misinterpreted is solved by using numerals for one and words for the other. Select the shorter word for convenience and write it out.

Don't use: 66 6-passenger planes, instead 66 six-passenger planes.
Don't use: 2 22-foot red carpets, instead two 22-foot red carpets.

When using short fractions, spell out the words: one-third, three-fourths. (You'll use figures when mixing fractions with whole numbers: $5^1/_2\%$ interest.)

Formal documents also invite spelled out numbers: invitations, legal papers, announcements.

The wedding will take place at two o'clock at the church on Seventh Avenue.

The dowry settlement amounts to Four thousand Fifty-two dollars ($4,052). (Lawyers prefer both written and spelled-out versions.)

NUMBERS IN DATES AND TIME

Dates are usually written with the month (spelled out), the day and the year (in numerals): June 5, 2000. The longer months can be abbreviated in tight places: Dec. 25, 1950.

Be careful writing only numerals to indicate a date. Some errors might occur because of a misinterpretation. In some locations, dates are written European style: 5 June 2000 or 25 December 1950 (note the lack of punctuation). When these dates are written in numerals, they become 6/5/00 and 12/25/50, or 5/6/00 and 25/12/50. The December date poses no problem since there isn't a 25th month. but the June date could be misinterpreted as May 6 (5/6) instead of June 5 (6/5). Make it easy on yourself. Write out the month, whichever order you use.

In business correspondence (and probably personal as well), it's a good idea to include the year at least once per document. Because files and records are stored for years, these complete dates could prevent a problem in the future. A municipal records keeper notes the importance of keeping the year complete (1935 as opposed to '35). In older communities, property listed as built in '85 could easily be 1785 or 1885. As we near the turn of another century, the problem is sure to be raised again.

Do not use the ordinal (*th, st, rd, nd*) form of numbers when writing the complete date: *January 15 is the date for the examination.* However, you may use the ordinal suffixes if you use only the day: *The 15th is the date for the examination.* Can't you hear Miss Miller reminding you that while you may pronounce it January 15th, you don't write the *th*.

Time is written in numerals (except in formal use) and is accompanied by a.m./p.m. or am/pm or AM/PM or A.M./P.M. Deciding on which form to use calls for a style manual.

Be consistent in using hour and minute figures. If you use 10:15 a.m., then use 2:00 p.m. If you don't need the minutes, use 10 a.m. and 2 p.m. Remain consistent throughout a piece of writing.

NUMBERS AND MONEY

Because much business writing pertains to money, invoices, payrolls and taxes, business people tend to use more numerals than short story writers. The same general rules apply: use figures for numbers above ten.

Most money figures are in numerals, particularly dollars and cents. Omit the decimal and two zeros when writing round dollar figures.

The bill amounted to $80. When the tax was added, it came to $84.29.

Cents alone are depicted as 34 cents and not as $.34 (unless in a column with many other numbers). That old symbol for cents (the c with a line through it) isn't even available on most word processors. If you're using a typewriter, try not to use it anyway.

Write big, big numbers in a combination of words and numerals: $5 million, $1.2 million, $2.25 billion. If the numbers are detailed into the thousands, go to all figures: $4,275,000 rather than $4,275 million.

Business writers, as a specific group, particularly like to mix the very big numbers with letters. They're easier to read: $2.5 million (instead of $2,500,000) and $45K (meaning $45,000). Some business people use the letter M to represent thousands; some use K.

Receipts from the emergency room topped the $150 million mark. That averaged out to about $1.25 million a month, or $40K for each patient.

WHEN TO USE NUMERALS

Measurements, weights, temperature readings, stock market quotes, percentages and addresses are written in numerals.

Measurements require numerals used with other symbols.

The size of the lot was 120' x 80'. The worker was hit on the head by a 2 x 4. He was taken to the hospital in his own 4X4 pickup.

Weights also require numerals, sometimes used with symbols.

The worker weighed more than 200 pounds, considerably more than the 4-pound, 3-ounce board. That was because he regularly carried 2 gallons of water on his back.

Temperature is written with numerals, either with degrees in word or symbol (°). Choose one and use it consistently throughout a document.

The poor fellow's fever ran up to 101.8 degrees. He stayed cool since the outside temperature was a mere 40°.

Stock Market quotes appear without decimals.

The blue chip stock closed at 32¼, off ½.

Percentages are also written in numerals, with the percent written out. Use the percent sign (%) only in tables, graphs and charts.

The fund drive raised 38 percent of its goal, with only .03 percent received from new donors. The sales quota was 25 percent higher than last year.

Numbered streets are usually written in numerals. Some exceptions suggest we write out numbered streets under ten. Street names above Tenth also call for ordinal numerals: 15th Street, 19th Place. House and apartment numbers always are written in figures.

The accident occurred on the corner of First Avenue and 45th Court. The victim lived at 105 45th Court, Apartment 6. The witness lived at 4516 First Avenue.

Highway and route numbers also are numeralized.

The way to the hospital was on Route 1 by way of State Highway 536.

ORDINALS AND CARDINALS

There seems to be a religious connotation to numbers, having to do with rank and position. They are referred to as ordinals or cardinals, and they come in denominations! Ordinals are the *st*, *nd*, *rd*, and *th* words (1st, 2nd, 3rd, 4th. Ordinal comes from the word meaning "to be ordained, to be put in order"). Cardinal numbers are the ones we use to count from one to whatever (1, 2, 3, 4. Cardinal means "principal, of basic importance").

Write out ordinal numbers when they contain just one word: third prize, tenth in line, sixtieth anniversary, fifteenth birthday. Use numerals for the others: the 52nd state, the 21st Amendment.

When all this is digested and committed to memory, a third grade logic will probably be the best guide you have in using numbers. Consistency is the key. As long as you are consistent, other people will figure you know what you're doing.

The use of numbers in business writing is probably the best selling point for providing offices with style manuals. Check out the many good ones available through book stores. Or, your office manager may decide to make up one for the entire office. However it is done, a style manual gives everyone within an organization the writing guidelines that result in consistency throughout the company. Style manuals save much unnecessary stewing.

EXERCISES

Consider developing a style manual to decide how you and your company use numbers. Answer the following questions—once and for all time.

1. How will dates be written? July 4, 1995 or 4 July 1995?
2. Will months ever be abbreviated? If so, when?
3. How is time written? What about am and pm?
4. What is the preferred way to refer to money amounts?
5. Do you write out percent (%) or degree (°) or use symbols?
6. Is punctuation used in computerized addresses?

(Add your own questions that pertain to your field of endeavor.)
7.
8.
9.
10.

19

What's Your Point?

Before anyone sits down to write, they need to have a message. More important, they need to have a clear message. The best way to do that is to take the time to consider, What's the point? What is the writer trying to convey. Here are some tips for setting writing objectives.

When you rushed home from third grade to tell your folks about how you learned to write, you were confused about what "learning to write" entailed. You defined it either as learning to write script, handling a pen on paper (remember the miles of scrolls and fence posts you practiced in penmanship class?) or as controlling the rules of grammar long enough to string a few sentences together.

Writing is some of that, of course. But it is so much more than forming letters and applying rules. Writing is communicating.

Writing is tapping into yourself and your ideas; writing is describing your emotions; writing is connecting yourself with the rest of the world; and writing is sending an idea to another person.

Writing is touching another soul, moving that soul to respond with an "Aha! so that's what you mean" or "Why didn't I think of that?" or "Isn't that beautiful!" or "Such words to express so much emotion."

As children, your reasons for writing were few: because you had to, because you had to, because you had to. It is the rare child who keeps a journal (diary) or writes to express their feelings.

PURPOSE

Knowing your reason for writing saves time and words when it comes to composing the message. Children will think long and hard about the purpose of their writing. After all, they wouldn't want to waste their time writing something that didn't fulfill the teacher's assignment!

As grownups, the reasons for writing are many: to transfer information; to request information, material, time, etc.; to persuade or sell; to touch base or make nice; or to document (cover your backside), because you have to.

Unfortunately, most adults just sit down and write. Somewhere near the end, if at all, a thought might appear about why the heck am I doing this? If that thought had been moved up front, the message would be much clearer. It's called putting the bottom line on top, a solid business strategy.

For beginners, consider the purpose of your writing the next time you sit down to compose. Am I simply providing data? Do I want something? Do I wish to change someone's mind? Am I expressing gratitude or maintaining contact? Is this for the record? By defining your purpose, you are one giant step closer to defining your point.

Too much business correspondence is composed like a mystery story. "I'll whet their appetites with innuendos so they'll be waiting for my bottom-line message," many grownup writers believe. In fact, the best business writing technique is just the opposite.

Why not begin with a purpose statement:

Here's the information you asked about.

I'm writing to ask you to appear at the company's next party.

Hey, friend, want to be rich, beautiful and famous overnight?

I'm writing to express my appreciation for your help last week.

The following is an account of our telephone conversation this morning about the new accounting system.

With this kind of straightforward writing, there are no doubts about what the document contains, thus saving the reader the time to sift through and guess. Busy business people appreciate this kind of message.

Bottom line? Put it on top!

This technique works well in providing information, responding to requests, making requests, and documenting.

CLOSINGS

Most people, when reading a letter, glance at the bottom to see what the writer wants them to do. Give your readers a surprise and provide them with that courtesy. Let your bottom line live with purpose.

More letters have been ruined by a namby-pamby closing than by any other part. If there is one sentence in the world that should be unlawful, it is this:

If you have any further questions please don't hesitate to ask.

Is there any doubt that a letter reader would hesitate if they had questions? Is there any doubt that the letter writer is trying to cover any oversights that may have been made?

Give your reader a break and use this valuable closing space to ask for what you want.

Call me with your ideas on this.
Let me know by Tuesday if you think this will work.
I need your response by noon on Friday.
Let's get together for lunch Monday to discuss this further.

Sometimes a summary of the letter is all that is needed in this valuable spot.

This should provide the information you need.
We always enjoy working with your company.
When you call, use my direct line at (999) 222-4321.
Please keep me updated when this occurs again.

Negative Messages

In responding to negative messages, a kinder, gentler approach is needed. We don't want to come out right away with such turn-downs as:

No, you didn't get the loan.
Your credit has been turned down.
You didn't get the job.
You failed the test.

Negative messages must be couched in a positive attitude. Somehow, the writer's responsibility is to soften the blow and offer encouragement. Only attorneys have the right to deliver negative messages with a direct blow.

Other tricky writing involves responding to negative messages, answering the complaints of customers or the dissatisfaction of a client.

In all of this negative kind of writing, some guidelines for softening the punch are challenging to apply. Strategies can be developed for this kind of message, and experts are surfacing in the field of responding to negative comments.

Negative messages need a sandwich construction. The bad news needs to be sandwiched between two positive pieces of news. It begins with a buffer, an opening that introduces the subject in a positive way.

Good credit is the backbone of today's economy.
In today's world, people need a strong line of credit.
The response to our ad for an office manager brought a deluge of mail.
Education is important.

A gold cup award ought to be provided for the personnel manager who can come up with a satisfactory response to a rejected job applicant. This may be the most difficult letter to write. Just the fact of the letter has told the recipient they are still unemployed.

Some very comforting letters have turned up, however, indicating that with a little thought, such negative responses are possible.

Closings for a sandwich-construction negative message involve an up-lifting, encouraging message that tells the recipient to keep trying.

Until financing can be arranged, you may want to consider our layaway plan. Perhaps this will help you.
Please contact us when you have fulfilled the credit requirements. We want you as a customer.
Be encouraged in your job search. You'll find just the right position to use your excellent skills.
The test will be repeated in three months. That should give you time to try again.

In between the positive pieces of bread, the negative message will lie protected and not so difficult to swallow. The goodwill that results is worth the effort to write such a message.

AUDIENCE

Once the purpose of your message is clear, good writers consider their audience. Who will be reading this message? The expected readers determine the tone of the writing, word choice, the degree of formality used. And the audience must be identified before the writing begins.

In business, the audience takes one or more of four directions.

Writing upstairs (supervisor, company chief, board of directors, boss of whatever label) will have a more formal tone, a more questioning tone. One may suggest and respond to, ask questions of, and relay information to a boss. One seldom orders or chastises in messages upstairs.

Writing downstairs (to staff, employees, work team, subordinate departments) allows more leeway in tone. A less formal atmosphere provides a comfortable way of writing. Because they understand, you can use technical terminology and abbreviated ideas to discuss what you have to. You can use a chastising tone or give orders, if you feel the need.

Writing inside (to other departments or divisions within your company) you can maintain that informal tone. However, you may want to make sure that readers in other departments understand your technical terms. Too often people in the Accounting Department assume that everyone speaks their language.

Writing outside (to clients, customers, suppliers, the world in general) is a challenge. A more respectful tone is appropriate, more formal language may be needed. Technical language should be kept to a minimum and used only when needed.

Each message must fit the reader, must set the tone for receiving the communication that you wish to send. In more formal occasions, the words will tend to be more formal. In situations concerning emotions, the words must be careful and sensitive.

Dear Boss: I've been sweating at this desk for almost six years now, and as yet I have never received one single word of appreciation. Slaves get a pat on the back once in awhile, but not me. It is time that I decided whether or not to stay chained to this desk another week. Therefore, if there aren't some words of appreciation and a matching pay increase in my next paycheck, I'm walking. Please give this your immediate consideration.

If the above letter were sent to a boss, the result most likely would be that the writer is out looking for a new job. To write upstairs requires tact, diplomacy, and soft words. Let's try this one again.

Dear Boss: I've been a loyal employee of this company for more than six years, and I enjoy the work. My records indicate that I have effectively carried out all my workload and more during this time. The records will also show that I have not had a pay increase in more than three years. Over these years, my duties have substantially increased and I feel I am worth more to the company now. Will you please review my records and request an increase in my pay to meet the quality of work I do?

A staff memo is much easier to write. After all, you're the boss and can use a sterner tone—if you wish. A good boss knows that listening to the staff is the best way to approach managing them.

Dear Staff: Now I realize that traffic is difficult in the mornings, that you spend countless hours gridlocked, and that your hands are tied as to alternatives. Still, our phones begin to ring at 8:30 A.M. with customers expecting answers to their questions. When you aren't at your phones, the customer must wait and be handled by someone else. What can we do to remedy this predicament? Let's meet in the conference room Friday at 3 P.M. to work out some way of finding a solution.

Notes you write to your family need to be as clear as possible, but the word choice is wide open.

Dear Honey, Wow! A year ago you didn't know how to cook a hotdog. Here you are, preparing a special dinner for the two of us tomorrow night. I'm impressed. I would just love it if you would fix that great ravioli sauce of yours for the pasta. You know how much I love it— and you.

The hardest letter to write is the one to the school principal or teacher. (You just know they're going to read it over for grammar construction and spelling!)

Dear Principal: Your responsibility for the safety and welfare of your students is top priority with you. I can see that, and I can understand how you must feel when a child like mine breaks the rules. I have been talking to him about the importance of safety, and he assures me he understands the need to walk when in the school building. He tells me he'll save his running until he's on the playground, or at home. Thank you for bringing this to our attention.

When you write with a very formal tone, you leave out as much personality as possible. This is a strictly business kind of endeavor, although it doesn't always have to be as stuffy as the following.

To the Board of Directors: Enclosed is the report you requested of this department following the last Board meeting. The survey was concluded within the week and has been quantified and graphed for ready understanding. Please notice the bottom-line summary presented in the opening pages. Detailed survey data is located in the appendix, with terminology definitions offered in footnotes and chapter annotations. Thank you for the opportunity to prepare this report for the Board.

Formal Writing

Formal writing, incidentally, is that which uses no contractions and avoids personal pronouns. When writing within a company, you may feel free to use all the I-me-my-our-us words that you wish. But, keep writing in the second or third person when writing outside the company.

Avoid contractions when writing official company reports, when writing upstairs (most of the time), and when writing to the outside world. While contractions have been used by some companies to increase their warm fuzzy feelings with customers, other companies like to keep business on a more formal basis.

Choosing the level of formality and the tone of the message is part of maintaining the company's image. Communications departments need to address this in any firm that uses a large amount of written material to reach customers. Hold classes, talk about image, talk about word usage, and talk about formal language. Several large companies solve the problem by creating a department that handles all written correspondence!

Terms of Endearment

Letter writing in business has been handed down generation after generation from the days of pens and inkwells. Attorneys and bankers did most of the early business writing, using their grandiose language with Spencerian flourishes of the pen.

Unfortunately, much of that ostentation persists in today's business correspondence. We begin letters with a stiff greeting, Dear Whoever, and close with eloquent gestures of cordiality, respectful courtesy and everlasting sincerity.

These terms of endearment are outdated, outmoded and outlived (never mind outlandish).

Why on earth would a person you don't know be addressed as *dear*? And why would you waste all that time when you've finished a letter deciding whether you feel cordial, respectful, sincere, warmly regarding, truly or very truly? Surely you have better things to do with your time!

Shed some fresh light on your business correspondence by using innovative openings. Try using something you feel like writing.

Yes, Mr. Arliss,
We can get that order out by Tuesday.
Good morning, Tom Shultz,
You're right, Jim,
Nobody wants to sit and wait for something as important as a new tractor.

Any of these openers are understandable to a reader. They draw the reader into the message you're sending. *Good morning* is appropriate because most mail is opened in the morning.

Many business letters open with a heading, much like the headline of a newspaper. This gives the reader an idea of what the letter is about. People using account, file or case numbers use them in the heading. It speeds communication.

Such headings might read:

Response To March 10 Letter Re: Case No AFD1234
Application For Next Year's Vacation
Reservations For Hotel Suite
Order for Material for Purchase Order #607

To further gain attention, you may want to bold-face or capitalize the headings. These work particularly well when you don't have the name of a person to address. By including numbers and references to previous letters, the mail opener gets an idea where to route this one.

When you are faced with the dilemma of writing a letter with no particular addressee, try using a department name or a job title.

Marketing Department
Purchasing Order Manager
Head of Complaint Department

Any help you can give the mail opening person will be appreciated. It may also speed up response to your letter.

Titles such as Mr. or Ms. bring up another problem. Today many people carry names that are not identified by gender—such names as: Pat, Terry,

Chris, even Michael, George, and Alex. If you are in doubt, omit titles such as Mr. or Ms. (they're extraneous in business anyway). Simply use the entire name. You can't go wrong.

Good morning, Terry Grasshopper,
Michael Nadroj,
Hello, Chris Chringel,

Use titles for women only if you know what they prefer: Mrs., Miss or Ms.

About the closing endearing terms. Omit them. Save yourself time and agony by concluding your letter, dropping down a few spaces and writing your name. Nobody will notice. If they do, they may commend you for being so practical. Remember what was said about the value of the closing thought? Don't water it down with innocuous niceties that seem so misplaced in business correspondence. Make your point and quit.

In short, good writing begins by stating a purpose, continues with strategic messages planned to carry out that purpose, and closes with direct, positive, meaningful closings that clearly state what happens next. All of this is directed toward the intended reader. Don't let them wonder what point you want to make.

Exercises

Arrange a check list to review before beginning a writing project. You may wish to include answers to such questions as the following:

What is the purpose for writing this?
Who will read it?
What strategy will I use to get my point across?
What's my strongest opening?
What's my strongest closing?
Is my language (word usage) compatible with my purpose? with my readers?
In a formal report, have I avoided the personal pronouns and the contractions?

20

Selling Your Ideas (Persuasive Writing)

Persuasive writing gets special attention here. The knack of selling an idea or a product with a written communication is highly prized in the business world. Since we all use this skill, it seems important enough to include in this chapter about style.

Writing a persuasive message has its own style which must capture the reader's attention, interest the reader, describe the idea/product, and ask the reader to buy it. Persuasive messages also benefit from mechanical emphasis.

If you're married, have a close friend, have ever held a job, or belong to an organization, you have done a selling job—for yourself. People who hold jobs selling products or services will tell you they have to sell themselves before they can sell their products.

Selling is a major part of the American economy, even though we often call it persuasion when applied to personal goals. Selling. Persuasion. All this amounts to is convincing people of something they may not have thought of by themselves.

Whether you're trying to persuade someone to buy your product, come around to your way of believing, or hire your services, the art of writing a strong, positive message is invaluable. You'll find it as easy as A-B-C-D.

The best model for persuasive writing is found in advertising copy. If you look closely at newspaper or magazine ads, you'll find they employ the same principles as radio and television commercials. Print ads must catch your eye from a page full of other printed material; commercials last only a few seconds and are gone. Advertising copywriters know they have to get their message across as quickly as possible.

Persuasive messages are different from other writing. While most business messages are expected or requested, persuasive messages are the kind that few expect and fewer request. Therefore, the first problem is to grab the attention of the reader.

A = Attention

To get the reader's attention on paper, you must be bold. You can use mechanical techniques—white space, bold face letters, italics—and you can use words, but they have to be different from the routine.

Somewhere near the upper left hand corner (considered the place most eyes fall when opening a letter) use your attention-grabber. You might use a heading that asks a question, quotes an authority, or makes an outrageous claim (it better be true).

Before you finish reading this letter, 20,000 children will fail a spelling test.

If trees could talk, they would ask for your protection.

Look No Further—I'm Your Next Assistant

If you could find a can-opener that doesn't rust, would you buy it?

All of these opening lines would catch the eye of someone who wasn't expecting such a message in the mail. In the commercials, a kid runs into the room, slamming the door and yelling, "Hey Mom, I'm home, and I got an A on my tooth report card!" That's enough to wake up any sleepy viewer—and it usually does.

But it takes more than a slamming door to grab the attention of a proud parent. Consumers need to know how the slamming door affects them.

B = Benefits

Parents worth their bruises will feel the glow of pride experienced by the mom whose kid received all A's—even on a tooth report card. She'll want to know how she can give her child the same benefits. That's the part that comes next.

At the same time you're grabbing your reader's attention, you need to know what the reader wants. Here's a tough one (unless you have a marvelous marketing organization that automatically provides lists of people in your target audience).

If you're writing to just one person, you may have a better idea of the interests that will do the trick. Does this person want fame, fortune, friends, or fun? What benefits will this person expect from your product/service/idea?

The mom watching the commercial about toothpaste isn't excited about dentifrice; she's excited about being considered a good parent.

You have to remember that McDonald's doesn't sell hamburgers. They sell convenience, economy, fast service, and family fun. Like McDonald's, you have to tell your reader how your product/service/idea is different from other fast food restaurants. In other words, why should your reader come to you?

Look again at the list of f-words a paragraph back. These are the reasons people change brands, buy services, or adopt ideas. If you're selling yourself to a prospective employer, you need to know if the company is looking for an employee who will give the company prestige, increase its income, be a team player, or show the company creative new programs.

If you're persuading someone to believe as you do, you first need to know which buttons will make it happen. Some people value tradition, the old ways; some are innovative and searching for new and better ways to do things. Which is the person you're communicating with?

C = CREDIBILITY

Once you have established contact, grabbed their attention and interested them in the benefits you're offering, you need to back up your claims.

Here is where you tell about the dentifrice or the double-cheeseburger. This is the place (in the middle of your written piece) that you describe the details of the contents, color, contrasts and costs of your product/service/idea. In a job application letter, this is where you preen your feathers and tell them how good you are and how you achieved your worth.

In a reasonable world, this should be the stuff that counts, the opening data, the information of importance. However important they are, and however necessary it is to include them, the details of your persuasive message need to be buried in the middle.

D = Do IT

The bottom line—literally—of a persuasive message contains the call to action. This is where you tell your reader that it's time to move, to do it! This is where the parent is told to run to the store now and pick up this toothpaste.

In the closing paragraph of a job application, you state positively that you're available for interviews or that you'll call in a few days to arrange a meeting.

This is the place you tell your reader how easy it is to be all they can be, to achieve all they want by responding now to your message. The closing must be strong and positive. Eliminate the *if* messages (If you like what you see, call me; if you want further information, call me; if you want to buy.) *If* messages are about as negative as you can get.

Know that all your persuasive talents rest on this closing and make it a good one.

Help those 20,000 children pass their next spelling tests by volunteering today.

If trees could talk, they would ask, "Please write your Congressional representatives today and ask them to vote No on the bill to destroy national parks."

Please let me know when we can meet to discuss ways my skills can meet your need for an assistant.

You can have this rust-free can opener in your home within 48 hours by calling the 1-800 number at the top of this letter. Don't wait; go to your phone now.

MECHANICAL HELP

Advertisers use a combination of pictures, graphics, colors, type fonts, sizes and shapes to get their messages across. You can give your persuasive writing a similar boost through mechanical means.

Caution: Don't go overboard with these. Use one or two of them, but not all at one time. Using all the mechanical aids is like using all the colors in the coloring box.

Typewriters and word processors provide a number of mechanical means for emphasizing a point or making a message stand out.

TRY USING ALL CAPS.

Underlining is another method of emphasis.

Use subheads to guide your reader.

Used sparingly, an exclamation point! or question mark? may help.

Bold-face letters help to bump up a message.

Italics makes ideas stand up and shout.

When providing several important points, try listing them:

A. Attention
B. Benefits
C. Credibility
D. Do it!

Bullets are useful in listing several ideas:

- Capitalized words
- Underlining
- Subheads
- Punctuation Marks
- Bold-face type
- Italics
- Lists (white space)

The secret to making words or phrases stand out is to put some white space around them.

If you write many persuasive/sales messages, become aware of advertising copy: the tricks of the trade. Notice what catches your eye, what turns you off, what makes you respond. You can be sure those are the things that will bring similar reactions from your readers.

P.S. Here's another secret: The P.S. after a closing signature is a grand place to put information you want noticed. Watch your own eyes! Don't you rush to read the P.S., sometimes before reading the letter?

EXERCISES

1. Select a newspaper, radio or television station, and write a letter supporting a stand they have taken or an opinion expressed.
2. Now write the same newspaper, radio or television station a letter contradicting a stand they have taken or an opinion expressed. Be as patient and persuasive as you can; yet, be strong enough to let the reader know you believe strongly in your point. Use the A-B-C-D method to arrange your ideas.
3. Review your letter(s) and enhance them with mechanical means—without overdoing it! Don't crowd. Don't preach. Don't rant. Don't give up.

21

Nonsexist Language

Sexism in language not only turns off many readers, but is illegal in some forms. Government agencies are presently requesting written materials to be free of sexism. How do we do that? Sexist language takes three basic forms. It assumes the world is masculine until proven otherwise; it demeans and diminishes with word endings; and it stereotypes. Here are some very basic ways to eliminate sexism in writing, but without reverting to the awkward *he/she* or the overuse of the word *person*.

The English language is a male-dominant language; terminology and words are weighted toward masculine usage. Today, this male-dominant language is called sexist if certain terms or words are assumed to apply equally to both sexes, but in fact do not.

Sexism in writing, particularly business writing, turns people off, personally, professionally, and legally. Great care must be taken to keep writing sexism-free, a topic Miss Miller couldn't even have dreamed of twenty years ago, and probably would have avoided because it means altering some of her precious rules.

Fortunately, it is not difficult to keep writing unbiased to gender.

Sexism takes three basic forms. First, it uses words that reflect the world as masculine; second, it demeans women by diminishing them with words; and third, it stereotypes roles with gender implications.

THE *MAN* WORDS

The assumption that the world is masculine until proven otherwise is reflected in *man* words, particularly the pronouns *he, him,* or *his* to refer to people whose genders are unknown. Grammatically, this is easy to correct by replacing the third person singular masculine pronoun *he* (such a long introduction for such a little word). This is a fairly simple process.

1. Change your writing to reflect first or second person singular (we, our, you, your).
2. Change your writing to reflect the plural third person (them, they).
3. Restate the sentence and use the offending information in a clause or phrase.
4. Rewrite the sentence passively to change the subject to object.
5. Eliminate the pronoun, replace it with the original noun, or replace it with the words *one* or *the*).

American language also utilizes many *man* words that once were expected to include women. Words like: mankind, salesman, businessman, penmanship, and phrases like: man of the hour, man hours, brotherhood of man, man the torpedos!

Words of this nature are easily replaced with words that more accurately describe the subject: civilization or humankind, sales representative or sales agent, executive or manager, writing ability, script, distinctive person, work hours, kinship of humans, go to war!

DIMINISH AND DEMEAN

The second form of sexism is found in diminishing and demeaning words, the kind of words that separate women from the standard *man* words, portray women as objects, possessions, or as little, less-than, second-class. Words like: waitress, bachelorette, actress, little woman, cookie, girl, aviatrix, or heiress.

When women are treated as less-than through language, the consequences follow in other parts of life—economically, politically, and academically. For centuries, women have not received the same educational opportunities that men have. Politically, women have been suppressed, overlooked and demeaned. Economically, the results of suppression have kept women in low-paying or non-paying work.

The word *girl* used in reference to a grown woman has probably done more to keep women in subservient positions than any other word. It implies incompetency, little-girl qualities, cuteness, and immaturity. When office people refer to the girls in Accounting or the girls in the front office, they are suggesting that these workers are not serious about their work and therefore don't deserve a woman's paycheck. And why not? For many years, women were not considered as a serious part of the workforce.

Use adjectives that point to women's abilities and strengths, not their weaknesses (or perceived weaknesses) or their appearance. When describing women workers, talk about their skills rather than how blond or how tall they are.

Use women's names on a par with the way all names are used in the office. For instance, don't call the boss Mr. Boss and a woman co-worker by her first name. Many women, who are called by their first names by men doctors, dentists, lawyers and stockbrokers, still have difficulty calling these men by their first names.

Do not use word endings that point to women as also-rans or objects. Eliminate the endings that say: the real word doesn't have this ending; this ending indicates only a woman. Use instead the words that best reflect the intended meaning.

adulteress	adulterer
barmaid	bartender
camera girl	photographer
chairwoman	chair
girl Friday	flunky/assistant
goddess	god
housewife	homemaker
	(has nothing to do with being a wife)
laundress	launderer
meter maid	meter reader
mistress of ceremonies	host
murderess	murderer
postmistress	post office manager
sculptress	sculptor
seamstress	sewer
spokeswoman	speaker
sportswoman	athlete
stewardess	flight attendant

STEREOTYPES

The third form of sexism is found in stereotyping certain words or ideals for women and men. Picture the following people in your mind's eye: bank president, lawyer, doctor, high school principal, teller, secretary, nurse, teacher. Did you picture the first four as men? The last four as women? That is stereotyping!

Women are entering all fields of endeavor and succeeding in them, proving to the world that places in government, the military, medicine, law, business, sports, religion, and the arts are places for women and men, working side-by-side.

Avoid referring to secretaries, nurses and teachers as *she* and to doctors, lawyers, executives as *he*. Keep an open mind about gender until you find out whether the company president is a man or a woman, the company secretary is a man or a woman.

Be careful to use appropriate titles when addressing letters. If a woman wishes to be addressed as Mrs. or Miss, she will say so. Otherwise, refer to her as Ms. Don't assume that the director of the traffic agency is a man or that the director of the health organization is a woman. If you have to use a title, find out which applies, or be neutral. If you don't have to use a title, don't.

Avoid referring to gender if it isn't necessary. Whether the lawyer is a woman or not probably isn't important. Know also that referring to her as a lady attorney or lady doctor is patronizing. First of all, it isn't important most of the time to make such a note. Secondly, the term lady is gratuitous. If she is a woman, say so. Don't hedge with alternative terms such as lady, gal, person or female.

By eliminating sexist language from your writing, not only will you be upholding the law, but you will be making friends, respecting people for who they are and what they do instead of whether they go to a hairdresser or a barber. (Many barbers count women as their clients; many hairdressers welcome men to their salons. They too are getting rid of gender and focusing on hair.)

Eliminating sexist language is not to suggest we eliminate sex or gender from our lives, just from our language.

EXERCISES
(Answers to exercises are in the Appendix.)

Review the following sentences and remove sexist language where it appears.

1. Barb must learn to curb her temper when appearing before the (all-male) board of directors.
2. Everyone should keep his cool when dealing with the Board.
3. Ken is only trying to be a gentleman where we girls are concerned.
4. "Yes, I like to open doors for you girls. That's the way I was taught."

5. If you ask me, Ken ought to ask Barb to marry him. Then she could stay home and keep house.

6. Maybe Ken could stay home and keep house. After all, Barbie does very well at her job for a woman.

7. This is the oldest argument of mankind.

8. Let's settle it now. Would you let your wife work, if you were married?

9. Could we get used to calling her Barbara Pease?

10. She'd probably use both names and become Barbara Warren-Pease.

Grammar Glitches

Sometimes grammar guidelines malfunction and you need some handy ways to write around them or adapt them to what you mean. Everybody—*everybody*—has words or phrases that they always have trouble with.

Do you capitalize government agency words, like city, state, federal? Do you capitalize family members, mother, father, aunt, uncle? When do you capitalize south, north, east, west? Where does the *s* belong in plural compound words (like brother-in-law, back-up)? What's the difference between its and it's?

Do I answer, "It is I" or "It is me"? How do I write a third person pronoun without being sexist? How do I address a letter to a person I don't know?

In this chapter, you'll identify some of those more common problem areas and find some easy-to-remember ways to solve them. Some of these are simple spelling problems: *ible* or *able*; *ac*cept or *ex*cept; *e*ffect or *a*ffect. Some are the old bugaboos of who or whom; like or as; likely, apt or liable. Some will address some ordinary problems of punctuation, such as whether or not to use an apostrophe. While many of the "problems" have been discussed in their corresponding chapters, this chapter provides a convenient review and reference.

ACCEPT/EXCEPT

If you accept a gift, you receive it, take it in. *Accept* is a verb that does something. *Except* is usually a preposition, meaning that something is left out. She ate everything on her plate except the potatos.

Affect/Effect

Both of these words can be either verbs or nouns. Most of the confusion stems from the verbs. The noun *effect* means a result, something that has been caused to happen. The noun *affect* is used rarely and has a meaning confined to psychology: an emotion or strong feeling.

As verbs, the two words have distinctive meanings. *Effect* means to bring about or accomplish. *Affect* means to change or alter, that is, to influence. The simplest test is to ask, can the word "influence" be substituted? If it can, use affect. If it can't, use effect. You'll be right most of the time.

I'm trying to effect a change in my eating habits.
This thing may affect my whole life.

All Told

The meaning of *all told* is everything taken into account. This is often misspelled *all tolled*.

Alright/All Right

Know the difference between *all right* and *alright, all ready* and *already, all together* and *altogether*. The single words are adverbs and modify verbs. (The band played alright. They were already playing advanced music. They played altogether well.) The combinations involve the pronoun all. The meanings show that all are right; all are ready; all are together.

Beside/Besides

In most usage, *besides* means in addition to, while *beside* means next to. Besides falling out of the race, the runner stayed beside the juice cart.

Between/Among

Between involves two things; *among* involves more than two. The argument was between the judge and the attorney; the jurors argued among themselves. There is a time to use *between* with more than two items: if you wish the items to be considered separately. The decision was between hanging the defendant, setting him free, or putting him in prison for life.

BOTH/EACH

These words are not interchangeable. *Both* refers to two things together; *each* can be any number taken one at a time. Both times we spoke, I told you about each of my children's activities.

CAN/MAY

Can I eat an apple? You may if you can! The words depend on permission. *Can* says you are able to; *may* says you have permission.

CAPS/AGENCIES

If you work for a government group, you probably will be asked to capitalize it (city, county, state, federal governments). Follow the advice given. Outside that agency, however, the words are not capitalized unless they're attached to capitalized names: Pierce County, New York City, Washington State.

CAPS/FAMILY

When talking about a family member and using an adjective modifier (generally a possessive: my, your, his, her) do not capitalize words like mother, father, brother, sister. If you do not use a modifier, capitalize the word as if it were a proper name.

She wanted to take her brother to the movies.
He wanted Father to take him. But Mother got the job.

CAPS/DIRECTIONS

Directions are capitalized only if they represent a specific place, such as the Northern Plains region, the Gracious South, the Wild West. Do not capitalize directions if they just point: drive east 15 miles, the house is three blocks north, we live on the west side of the intersection.

COMPARED TO/WITH

When you are showing a similarity between two ideas or things, use *compare to*. When you are examining, looking closely at people or objects, use *compare with*.

COMPLIMENTARY/COMPLEMENTARY

Easy to remember if you look at the letter that changes the meaning. *Complimentary* (with an *i* such as that found in praise) means to say nice things about someone. *Complementary* (with an *e* such as found in complete) means to add to, to make complete.

COMPOUND PLURALS

Compound words are made plural in two ways. If the first word is a noun, attach the plural to it: brothers-in-law, fights-royal, gentlemen-personified. If the first word is a modifier, attach the plural at the end: back-ups, brain-storms, bench-marks.

CONTINUAL/CONTINUOUS

Continual means recurring from time to time. *Continuous* means without interruption. So make up your mind. Is this a continual nuisance or a continuous pain in the backside?

COUNCIL/COUNSEL

A *council* is a noun referring to a group. *Counsel* is a verb meaning to provide guidance, and a noun meaning the advice given or the advisor giving it.

CREDIBLE/CREDITABLE

Look closely when you meet one of these words. Is the word *credit* in there? If it is, you mean that something is worthy of credit. *Credible* simply means believable. *Credulous*, on the other hand, is an adjective meaning gullible, believing everything you're told.

DISINTERESTED/UNINTERESTED

These words have two separate meanings. *Disinterested* means to be impartial, without interest for yourself. *Uninterested* means to be without any interest at all, bored. A psychologist must be a disinterested listener, but not an uninterested one.

EXCESS/ACCESS

Excess is too much; *access* is a way inside. After gaining access to the banquet table, he ate in excess of his appetite.

FARTHER/FURTHER

Use farther when indicating distance. Use further when you mean more. If you wish to discuss this further, we'll have to move farther into my office.

FLAMMABLE/INFLAMMABLE

A conundrum in the world of language. Both these words mean the same thing!

FORMALLY/FORMERLY

Two adverbs that get mixed up in pronunciation. *Formally* means to wear a tuxedo and be stiff; *formerly* means once upon a time.

GOOD/BAD

In a crazy upside-down world, good sometimes means bad, and bad means good. These words must be defined in context to the way they're used. Normally, they are adjectives. Slang has given them interchangeable meanings.

HARD/DIFFICULT/ARDUOUS/TEDIOUS/TROUBLESOME

If you think the work you do is hard, look again at the shades of meaning to the words above. Most of the time *hard* and *difficult* are interchangeable. However, if a task requires special skills to deal with complex details, it may be *difficult*. If the task requires physical or mechanical labor, it may be *arduous* or *tedious*; if a task is a cause for stress or worry, it may be *troublesome*. Consider the difference between *hard* (durable, sturdy, firm) and *difficult* (arduous, tedious, troublesome.).

HE (MEANING ANYONE)

Don't use the third person masculine pronoun *he* when you don't know the gender of the noun it replaces. If you don't know or are unsure, use any of the alternatives mentioned in Chapter 21. Or, use the third person plural. Avoid: Anyone wishing to go may bring his friend. Instead: Anyone wishing to go may bring their friend.

Ible/Able

How do you decide which suffix to use? If you can complete your word with the suffix *ation*, use *able*. Try ending your word with such suffixes as *ive, tion*, or *ion*. If that works, use *ible*. This works enough of the time to be useful.

Infer/Imply

It takes two people to infer and imply. The do-er implies; that is, the do-er suggests or hints at something. The do-ee infers; that is, draws a conclusion. A speaker implies; a listener infers.

Insure/Ensure/Assure

These three words are close enough in meaning to be interchangeable. *Ensure* carries slightly lighter shading of legally guaranteeing. *Insure* stresses taking necessary measures ahead of time. *Assure* means to remove doubt and suspense.

Its/It's

The difference between *its* and *it's* is more than an apostrophe. *Its* (without an apostrophe) is a possessive: its fur, its surface, its value. *It's* (with an apostrophe) is a contraction of it is. It's that simple!

It Is I/It Is Me

Because the verb *is* functions as a linking verb, the words on either side of it must complement each other. If one word isn't an adjective, that is, a description of the other, then both words must play the same role (complements). Since *it* is a subject (Column A words), then the pronoun complementing it must also be a Column A word, a subject. *I* is found in Column A; *me* is found in Column B. You decide! (You're right, it is I.) Now that you know the grammar, you may use the idiom "It's me" without guilt.

LEAVE/LET

Leave means to allow something to stay where it is. *Let* means to grant permission. *Leave me alone* means to allow me to be alone. *Let me alone* means to get off my back.

LEND, LOAN, BORROW

While *lend* and *loan* are nearly interchangeable, *loan* is generally confined to finance. I'll lend you my typewriter if you'll loan me $20. Borrow applies to the action of taking the loan. Give me the $20 and you can borrow my typewriter.

LIKE
(N/ADJ/ADV/V/PREP/CONJ/INTERJ)

An interesting word in that it may be used as any one of seven functions of language: noun, adjective, adverb, verb, preposition, conjunction, or interjection.

Rae had distinct likes and dislikes. (noun)
She preferred elegant clothes of like designs. (adjective)
She likely wore them for everyday wear. (adverb)
If Rae liked a jacket, she might buy it on impulse. (verb)
Her appearance was like a fresh breeze in stylish circles. (preposition)
People thought she was fashionable, like a movie star. (conjunction)
They adored Rae, like for real! (interjection)

LIKE/AS

The challenge of these words is deciding whether to use a preposition or a conjunction. *Like*, while it can be many different parts of speech, is often used as a preposition and is normally followed by a noun or pronoun, not by a clause.

This project seems like a snap.
You look like a tree.
The freedom of a bird is like a soaring updraft.

As, on the other hand, most often functions as a conjunction and introduces a clause. It sometimes requires additional words: *as if* or *as though* or *as . . . as*.

This project can be done as if it were a game.
You look like a tree as you stand against the sunset.
You are as free as if you were a bird soaring above the trees.

LIKELY/APT/LIABLE

Likely means probable. (The play is likely to begin on time.) *Apt* indicates a strong tendency. (The actors are apt to over-emote.) *Liable* predicts a bad ending. (The play is liable to draw strong criticism.)

PAST/PASSED/PASTIME

The confusion here is in the sound of the words. Both *past* and *passed* are pronounced alike. *Past* is a noun or adjective that means over and done with. *Passed* is the past tense of the verb to pass. (She passed the line of modesty in one of her past lives.) *Pastime* is a single word, not a compound.

PERSECUTE/PROSECUTE

One can persecute (bring suffering to) without a lawyer. One can only prosecute if one goes to court.

PRINCIPAL/PRINCIPLE

Principal, which can be a noun or an adjective, means chief, whether it's a person or a description. Remember how Miss Miller tried to convince you that a principal was a pal? *Principal*, another pal, refers to a capital sum of money that is placed at interest or used as a fund. *Principle* refers to rules of conduct. (Note that *rules* and *principles* both end in les.)

RAISE/RISE

Somebody somewhere has to do the work of raising something. Something that rises does so by itself. You can raise the roof if you like, but the sun will rise tomorrow as usual.

SHORT
(N/ADJ/ADV/V)

Short is another word that can be used in many functions of language: noun, adjective, adverb, verb.

The short was noted in the year-end inventory. (noun)
The materials were in short supply. (adjective)
The entire process fell short of its goal. (adverb)
"Don't you ever try to short me again," the owner shouted. (verb)

SIT/SET

When one sits, one puts one's bottom on a chair, bench, sofa, or other piece of furniture. When one sets, one has to have something in one's hand. In other words, you may set the chair in the middle of the room before you sit on it. Used this way, *sit* is a stop action verb (not requiring an object). *Sit* can also be used as an action verb, meaning to cause to be placed in a seat, as in: The maitre d' will sit the couple near the window. This verb, which requires an object, often uses a reflexive as in: Sit yourself at any empty table.

THAT/WHICH/WHO

The difference between *that, which*, and *who* is apparent when we realize that *who* refers to persons and *that* and *which* refer to anything else. A more subtle difference occurs between *that* and *which*. While these pronouns are interchangeable most of the time (when referring to things), the word *that* has a significant use to indicate an identifying clause. When a clause seems to demand the use of *that* rather than *which*, you can leave out the commas; you have a necessary clause.

TOWARD/TOWARDS

However much some grammar technicians may try to muddy up these words, they both mean the same. They are interchangeable.

WAITING FOR/ON

When you are expectant, holding your breath, daring hardly to move, you are waiting for. When you are serving another person with food, slippers or reading glasses, you are waiting on.

WHO/WHOM/WHOSE

These pronouns fall in Columns A, B, and C of the Handy Dandy Pronoun Guide. *Who* is found in Column A, as a subject. *Whom* is found in Column B, an object. *Whose* is found in Column C as a possessive. (See Chapter 2 for more on who and whom.)

The victim was one who liked to take risks.
The accident occurred to the daredevil whom they chose to drive.
Whose fault was it, really?

Appendix

ANSWERS

(Preferences of the author)

NOUNS—CHAPTER 1

1-1. An advertising agency in Chicago is called Syntax, Inc.

1-2. The special clients of Syntax are manufacturers in the city of Chicago.

1-3. When the company president James Valdez needed more help, he placed an ad in the *Wall Street Journal*.

1-4. Who knew the governor would seek a position as his communications director?

1-5. Only one person at the agency knew that the governor was a friend of President Valdez.

1-6. The client *lists* were divided between *attorneys* and computer *companies*.

1-7. The account *execs* often ate *tomatos* in the board room using steak *knives*.

1-8. They discussed *data* for the *write-ups* contained in the file *indexes*.

1-9. This information helps *agencies* provide the *media* with better *analyses*.

1-10. The *clients* considered the *processes* as valuable *assets* to their *services*.

1-11. Valdez' birthday is tomorrow.

1-12. James' mother is the founder's sister.

1-13. There are three Jameses in Syntax's company.

1-14. The new executive should be here in a week's time.

1-15. Each one's anticipation must be kept in check.

Challenge: If an apostrophe were placed between the N and S, the driver would have a 3-year-old (my son is 3).

PRONOUNS—CHAPTER 2

2-1. Who's
2-2. him
2-3. she
2-4. she
2-5. me
2-6. us, we
2-7. I
2-8. her
2-9. himself
2-10. him
2-11. has, do
2-12. himself, him
2-13. he (if you mean James), they (if you mean the onlookers)
2-14. are
2-15. are
2-16. I, are
2-17. whoever, it, their
2-18. she, is
2-19. one, us, ourselves, we, our, we (or—one, them, themselves, they, their, they)

VERBS—CHAPTER 3

3-1. The president holds interviews in the cafeteria.
     The president held interviews . . .
     The president will hold interviews . . .
3-2. The president has held interviews . . .
     The president will have held interviews . . .
3-3. The president is holding interviews . . .
     The president was holding interviews . . .
     The president will be holding interviews . . .
3-4. The president does hold interviews . . .
     The president did hold interviews . . .
3-5. Hold interviews in the cafeteria!
3-6. If the president were to hold interviews, they'd be in the cafeteria. (wishing)

If the president was to hold interviews in the cafeteria, they'd be . . . (stating)

3-7-a. evoke, evoked, will evoke
has evoked, will have evoked
is evoking, was evoking, will be evoking
does evoke, did evoke
Evoke any kind of response you can!

3-7-b. interviews, interviewed, will interview
has interviewed, will have interviewed
is interviewing, was interviewing, will be interviewing
does interview, did interview
Interview thirty-two prospects, James!

3-7-c. plays, played, will play
has played, will have played
is playing, was playing, will be playing
does play, did play
Play the games involved in greeting a new associate!

3-8. Whatever is needed to keep this office operating forever and ever until the end of time is to be done absolutely and as quickly as possible.

3-9. can, had, is, work, writes (if she still does it), or wrote (if she no longer does it)

3-10-a. had lost

3-10-b. will have spoken

3-10-c. will have announced

3-10-d. prepared, will prepare; Prepare the evaluation . . .

3-10-e. will display

3-11. The Board received the qualifications before the meeting.
James Valdez explained the voting procedures to the Board.
Valdez read aloud the qualifications.
The finance officer delivered recommendations to the Board following the reading.

3-12. The board had controlled the accounting staff for years.
This action has driven several of the accountants to leave their jobs.
The board honored the accountant's decision.
This, of course, will create an opening in the department.
When the search is finished, the director will have listened to 50 interviews.
This project developed in several distinct phases.

We had hoped to fill the position by mid-year.
Change the rules if you will; this is the board's position.

ADJECTIVES—CHAPTER 4

4-1. All the experienced candidates were qualified.

4-2. Two of them—the illustrious Kenneth Pease and the enterprising Barbara K. Warren—stood out.

4-3. The enthusiastic Board members were in agreement.

4-4. The puzzled staff wondered about the decision.

4-5. The eager President Valdez encouraged the methodical Board to choose one dynamic candidate.

4-6. fewer

4-7. This

4-8. These

4-9. more, fewer

4-10. furthest

4-11. Two final candidates could cause a head-on collision among the already-perplexed Board members.

4-12. Several do-it-yourself suggestions were made as tie-breakers.

4-13. No one considered a do-or-die quick decision.

4-14. Let's just take one more raised-hand vote.

4-15. The Board decided to hire both top-notch candidates in one rash go-to-hell unanimous vote.

ADVERBS—CHAPTER 5

5-1. Kenneth Pease was seeking an extremely high quality advertising agency.

5-2. He positively knew he wanted high standards.

5-3. In reality, he preferred a vastly prestigious agency.

5-4. He enthusiastically directed his efforts toward Syntax.

5-5. Would he wind up exceedingly bored at a smaller agency?

5-6. likely

5-7. reckless

5-8. wholeheartedly

5-9. hardly

5-10. scarcely

5-11. wrong

5-12. directly

5-13. straight

5-14. high

5-15. closely

5-16. The president of Syntax agreed in an enthusiastic way to hire both candidates.

5-17. The candidates graciously accepted the dual offer of the Board.

5-18. The time was set by Valdez for a day suitable to all of them to begin work.

5-19. He spread the news secretly to Elizabeth and Tony before announcing to the company.

5-20. The company looked forward hopefully to meeting their new associates soon.

PREPOSITIONS—CHAPTER 6

6-1. Most *of the people* (adj.) *in the room* (adj.) had a healthy attitude *about meeting the candidates* (adj.) who were *about* (adv.) *to arrive* (i. v.). Many whispered restlessly *among themselves* (adv.). Small groups huddled *up* (v.a.) *to each other* (adv.), sharing thoughts *among themselves* (adv.). Kenneth Pease arrived first, swaggering boldly *into the crowd* (adv.) waiting *at the door* (adv.). He waved gallantly, smiled broadly and shook hands *with the president* (adv.) *of the company* (adj.). When Barbara Warren, who pulled *up* (v.a.) *in a stretch limo* (adv.), rose *to speak* (i.v.), she caused a hush *to fall* (idiom) *over the audience* (adv.). Her appearance was stunning, *like a breath* (adv.) *of fresh air* (adj.). Her hair was loosely tied *in the back* (adv.) and her clothing resembled an Eastern princess. Did she dare *to think* (i.v.) she would be able *to convince* (i.v.) anyone she was an executive?

6-2. into

6-3. for

6-4. to

6-5. for

6-6. from

6-7. both

6-8. off

6-9. to

6-10. All

6-11. to

6-12. Why did you bring up that dilemma we didn't want to work out of?

6-13. Barbara, an avid football enthusiast, expounded during the Monday coffee break. The *down*-and-dirty (adj.) opposition are expected to pull a *downer* (n.) before the game. They probably arrive *down* (adv.) in the locker room wearing their *down* (adj.) jackets and demanding successions of first *downs* (n.). They ought to get *down* (adv.) on their knees and hope the players *down* (v.) the ball before the third *down* (n.) or they won't get *down* (prep.) the field to the touch*down* (adj.) line. They probably couldn't afford even the *down* (adj.) payment on a football. If they were to shout, "*Down* (v.) with the tyrants!" you might assume they were *down* (v.) on the opposition, not forcing something *down* (prep.) the throats of their own team.

CONJUNCTIONS & EXPLETIVES—CHAPTER 7

7-1. because
7-2. and
7-3. although
7-4. while
7-5. yet
7-6. but
7-7. Both, and
7-8. so that
7-9. both, and
7-10. since
7-11. "Indeed, your idea is definitely on the right track," said Elizabeth.
7-12. "Hey, your remark was unnecessary," returned Barbara.
7-13. "Yippee! You couldn't have thought of anything better," put in Ken as he tossed her a yellow pad.
7-14. "Darn! I dropped it," yelled Barbara.
7-15. "I feel a bit warm in here."
7-16. "Not a breeze of air conditioning is stirring in the room."
7-17. "I think I'll give up and go to my office," said Elizabeth.
7-18. "A pile of work is waiting for me."
7-19. "Summer is the warmest season of the year," suggested Ken.
7-20. "Possibly we could rig up a fan," retorted Barbara.

VERBALS—CHAPTER 8

8-1. *Building a reputation* (G) is important.
8-2. For years she wanted *to enhance her own reputation* (I).
8-3. *Thinking it was easy* (G) aided in *producing the visual image first* (G).

8-4. Little did she know, *looking good* (G) and *being good* (G) are two different things.

8-5. Her goal was *to start off the job* (I) with a bang.

8-6. To get along with Barbara

8-7. to make friends

8-8. to choose the desk near the door.

8-9. to move the furniture, to help.

8-10. to help

8-11. *Determined to do this job* (P), she accepted his help.

8-12. *Outnumbered* (S), he also had caught the fix-up fever.

8-13. *Excited at the prospect* (P), the two set to work the next Saturday morning.

8-14. They had worked four hours before they stopped to rest, *resolved to finish in one day* (P).

8-15. They actually enjoyed the hard work, *delighted with the joy of working together* (P).

8-16. The office had a new coat of paint applied by the executives.

8-17. Inspired with creativity, they had painted over some bare spots.

8-18. The room looked messier by the minute after they kicked over the paint can.

8-19. Feeling tired, they admitted that one side of the office didn't look as good as the other.

8-20. The janitor saw that the painters, having finished by late Saturday, spattered paint on each other.

COMMAS—CHAPTER 9

9-1. The next weeks, apart from small squabbles, passed uneventfully.

9-2. Barbara settled into doing what she does best, selling.

9-3. Kenneth, attempting to appear nonchalant, bypassed Barbara at every chance.

9-4. Of course, James Valdez believed he had made an impeccable choice.

9-5. "Yes, Elizabeth, Ken and Barb are working well together," he was heard to remark. Or: "Yes Elizabeth, Ken and Barb are working well together," he was heard to remark.

9-6. "If you listened, surely you'd come to the same conclusion," he told her.

9-7. Every sale carried a triple bonus: a cash percentage, gift certificates, luggage and a vacation in the Caribbean.

9-8. Working at Syntax less than two months, Barb had overtaken Ken and, would you believe it, shot out ahead.

9-9. While handling three clients at a time, Ken contrived to work on the annual report due in six weeks.

9-10. Furthermore, he redecorated their office using fourteen 1 x 6 shelves which carried books weighing up to 76 pounds, 6 ounces.

9-11. By the end of six months, Ken had moved into a new apartment at 123 Maple Street, Chicago, IL 99900.

9-12. On the other hand, Barb was still rooming with an old college friend, Skipper Hoover.

COLONS, SEMICOLONS & PERIODS—CHAPTER 10

10-1. Barb began considering a vacation trip to several places: Siam, Australia, New Zealand, Fiji or New Guinea.

10-2. Travelers reported complimentary things about these places, such as, "I was delighted with the weather as well as the people."

10-3. Ken remarked, "I always wanted to loaf on a tropical beach."

10-4. "I want to relax in the sun from about 9:30 in the morning to 3:30 in the afternoon," Barb told him.

10-5. "By noon the first day, you'd resemble the book *Bacon in the Sun* with the subtitle, 'Burned To a Crisp.' "

10-6. Don't try to approach; a snarling Ken needs quiet mornings.

10-7. Barb tries to protect him with a buffer.

10-8. She's the buffer; she screens his calls and callers.

10-9. Another clue: she likes to bring him donuts and coffee at 10:00.

10-10. When the weather turns cold, she switches to hot cocoa. (or ;) Ken likes cocoa better than chocolate.

10-11. She has taken to calling him by a special name, Pet. Hey, that could be considered "petty".

10-12. Ken is now considering taking his bonus vacation alone, all alone.

10-13. He's looking at places like Vienna, Austria; Lucerne, Switzerland; Athens, Greece; Amsterdam, Holland; or Papeete, Tahiti.

10-14. I'd expect Barb to throw a tantrum at that, one of her finest.

10-15. Not unless they know something we don't, which is possible.

QUESTION & EXCLAMATION MARKS—CHAPTER 11

11-1. Why would they want to throw us off with their antics?

11-2. Why, indeed? is my comment.

11-3. Never add unnecessary words to a sentence, never!

11-4. Surely that bothers you, doesn't it?

11-5. You bet it does!

11-6. If we wait, will their antics change?

11-7. Obviously you haven't seen the movie, "The Art of Being Artful."

11-8. Where, oh where, can I find a video tape copy?

11-9. Ken and Barb will be back from their vacations soon, anyway.

11-10. Then, of course, we'll have the answers to where, what, why, and whatever, won't we?

PARENTHESIS, BRACKETS & QUOTATION MARKS—CHAPTER 12

12-1. I found a copy of that video, "The Art of Being Artful."

12-2. "Did it provide clues to our friends' behavior?" asked Elizabeth.

12-3. Tony responded, "No, not a bit."

12-4. My postcard from Tahiti simply said, "Having a gooood (her word) time, glad you're not here."

12-5. Tony was speechless (a rare experience for him).

12-6. Let's list the facts: 1) Ken and Barbara are both on vacation. 2) They both headed for the South Pacific. 3) We've had only one postcard from Barb.

12-7. The conclusion (shades of Sherlock Holmes) is they must be together.

12-8. "We don't know that," Tony found his voice.

12-9. "Look, the postcard has a P.S.," Jeanette interjected. "It says 'Tahihi [sic] is terrific. KP.' "

12-10. "That says it all." Elizabeth smiled and returned to her office. "She knows more than she's telling," said Jeanette.

APOSTROPHES, ELLIPSIS, HYPHENS, DASHES, DIAGONALS—CHAPTER 13

13-1. In a week's time, Barb and Ken returned, sun-tanned, to their office.

13-2. You could see the vacation's effect on them both.

13-3. Barbara dove into her stacked-up work; Ken began calling on badly-neglected clients.

13-4. It's evident they missed their work.

13-5. It's also evident they didn't miss its concentration.

13-6. Where else could they get a tan like that—the Caribbean?

13-7. Everyone missed having them around—the bickering, in-fighting, double entendres.

13-8. "Let's get some work done around here," suggested James, the boss.

13-9. "We need a new campaign for the ultra-new Banks account—one of the most over-sold, under-publicized accounts in the country," James challenged them.

13-10. "They're eager to see what we'll come up with," he added.

13-11. ac-com-mo-da-tion
mer-ri-ment
sat-is-fac-tion
se-cu-ri-ty
right
ac-count
safe-ty
re-li-abil-i-ty
con-ve-nience
bank-ers

WORDS—CHAPTER 14

14-3-a. Ken's acting was good enough to qualify him for the leading community theater role.

14-3-b. The play called for family home type stage props.

14-3-c. Ken was told about three rules.

14-3-d. One was that sets damaged by the players are to be repaired.

14-3-e. Another was that repertory players could handle a variety of roles by keeping records.

14-3-f. Between September and December, Ken performed in four plays.

14-4-a. Meanwhile, Barb took figure skating lessons and was getting better each time.

14-4-b. The company was involved in reviewing the small print of her contract.

14-4-c. The board members believed that her risk of injury is a detriment to the company.

14-4-d. Steps must be taken to remove her from this activity.

14-4-e. Refer to the event three weeks ago when she suffered a knee injury that kept her off her feet for two days.

14-4-f. The board should take the appropriate action to determine if she should be allowed to continue.

14-4-g. By acting now, we can decide.

SENTENCES—CHAPTER 15

15-1. A robber took all the money from the lone clerk in the corner deli last night.

A robber took all the money from the corner deli last night; the clerk was alone.

A robber, holding up the corner deli last night, took all the money from the lone clerk.

15-2. Joe Bird, director of the Department of Fisheries, issued a new, harsh regulation.

The Department of Fisheries issued a new, harsh regulation; Joe Bird is the director.

The Department of Fisheries, directed by Joe Bird, issued a new regulation that many consider harsh.

15-3-a. The restaurant in a tough part of town was cited for cleanliness.

15-3-b. Most people on leave of absence who don't want to work offer too many excuses.

15-3-c. A long line of people is visible approaching the soup kitchen from the south.

15-3-d. We intended to spend all day working and helping out in the kitchen which holds 50 people.

15-3-e. By the end of the day, the food that we had cooked went to all the street people.

15-4-a. The firefighter didn't carry a hatchet, which was dangerous.

15-4-b. Three windows were broken in the fire and two people found themselves carried down the ladders.

15-4-c. All the residents escaped injury. However, a tired firefighter was overcome by smoke.

15-4-d. A fire like this can start only in the stairwell.

15-4-e. Out of the ashes, which are still smoldering, will rise a new building.

15-5-a. Ken and Barb realized they felt their lives were not useful.

15-5-b. They knew they could read in the paper what they believed was the reality of the world around them.

15-5-c. They thought they might do something useful with their time away from work.

15-5-d. Could they be useful if they took classes to learn to be socially responsible?

15-5-e. Both of them resolved to look at the options if they should decide to expand their horizons.

NONSEXIST LANGUAGE—CHAPTER 21

21-1. Barb must learn to curb her temper when appearing before the board of directors.

21-2. Everyone should keep their cool when dealing with the Board. We ought to keep our cool when dealing with the Board.

21-3. Ken is only trying to be a gentleman where we women are concerned.

21-4. "Yes, I like to open doors for women. That's the way I was taught."

21-5. (Eliminate remarks of this nature.)

21-6. Maybe Ken could stay home and keep house. After all, Barbara does very well at her job.

21-7. This is the oldest argument of humankind. (in the universe/of all time)

21-8. (The implication that one person can allow or not allow another to do anything is unacceptable in a free society.)

21-9. (Why must she change her name?)

21-10. The choice to assume another's name must be made by the people involved. And why Warren-Pease and not Pease-Warren?

Resource List

DICTIONARIES

Soukhanov, Anne, Editor, *American Heritage Dictionary of the English Language,* 3rd ed., American Heritage Publishing Co., Inc. and Houghton Mifflin Company, New York, 1992. Good inclusive usage help.

Oxford English Dictionary, 20 vols., 2nd ed., Oxford University Press, New York, 1986. For the serious dictionary owner.

Random House Webster's College Dictionary, Random House, Inc., New York, 1991. Includes some inclusive language.

Webster's Ninth New Collegiate, Merriam-Webster Inc., Springfield, MA, 1990. Traditional.

GRAMMAR TEXTS (HEAVY)

Barry, Robert E., *Business English for the '90s,* Prentice Hall, New York, 1989

Claiborne, Robert, *The Roots of English,* Random, New York, 1989

GRAMMAR TEXTS (LIGHT)

Gordon, Karen Elizabeth, *The Transitive Vampire,* Times Books, a division of Random House, New York, 1984. Fun while you learn.

Safire, William, *Fumblerule: Number Twenty: Verbs Has To Agree With Their Subjects,* Doubleday, New York, 1990. Or any other Safire book.

Strumpf, Michael & Douglas, Auriel, *Painless Perfect Grammar,* Monarch Press, New York, 1985. You'll smile through the pain.

Venolia, Jan. *Write Right,* Periwinkle Press, Woodland, CA, 1979. A handy quick guide.

NONSEXIST LANGUAGE

Dumond, Val, *Elements of Nonsexist Usage,* Prentice Hall, New York, 1991. Background to sexist language; guidelines to nonsexist language.

Maggio, Rosalie, *The Nonsexist Word Finder,* The Orynx Press, Phoenix, AZ, 1987. An extensive selection of alternatives.

PUNCTUATION

Gordon, Karen Elizabeth, *The Well-Tempered Sentence,* Ticknor and Fields, New York, 1983. Whacky, outrageous, instructive.

Shaw, Harry, *Punctuate It Right!,* HarperCollins, New York, 1986. Concise and useful.

SPELLING

Bolander, Donald O., *New Webster's Spelling Dictionary,* Grolier, Inc., Danbury, CT, 1987

Dougherty, Margaret M., *Instant Spelling Dictionary,* 3rd ed., Warner Books, New York, 1990

Grambs, David, *Death By Spelling,* Harper & Row, New York, 1989. Only for the strong-of-heart ambitious speller!

Lewis, Norman, *Dictionary of Correct Spelling,* Harper & Row, New York, 1962

Nurnberg, Maxwell, *I Always Look up the Word "Egregious,"* Prentice Hall, New York, 1981. Wit, common sense, helpful.

STYLE MANUALS

Associated Press Stylebook & Libel Manual, rev. ed., Addison-Wesley, Redding, MA, 1987

Chicago Editorial Staff, *Chicago Manual of Style,* 13th, rev., enl. ed., University of Chicago Press, Chicago, IL 1982

Lippman, Thomas W., compiler, *Washington Post Deskbook on Style,* 2nd ed., McGraw, New York, 1989

New York Times Manual of Style and Usage, Random, New York, 1982

THESAURUSES

Bolander, D., *New Webster's Thesaurus,* Grolier, Danbury, CT, 1986

Chapman, Robert L., *Roget's International Thesaurus,* 5th ed., HarperCollins, New York, 1992. The full-length, comprehensive version.

The New American Roget's College Thesaurus, New American Library, New York, 1962. A compact, carry-around version.

Random House Thesaurus Staff, *Random House Thesaurus College Edition,* Random, New York, 1984

WRITING STYLE

Barnett, Marva T., *Writing For Technicians,* Delmar Publishers, Inc., Albany, NY, 1982

Beardsley, Monroe C., *Writing With Reason,* Prentice Hall, Englewood Cliffs, NJ, 1976. Logic applied to writing.

Bernstein, Theodore M., *The Careful Writer,* Atheneum Press, New York, 1965. Or any other Bernstein book.

Freeman, Morton S., *A Treasury For Word Lovers,* ISI Press, Philadelphia, PA, 1983. A treasury of word information.

_____ *Words To the Wise: The Wordwatcher's Guide to Contemporary Style & Usage,* NAL Dutton, New York, 1991

Goldberg, Natalie, *Writing To the Bone,* Shambhala Publications, Boston, MA 1986. For the writer.

_____ *Wild Mind,* Bantam, New York, 1990. More help for the writer.

Lesikar, Raymond V., *Basic Business Communications,* Richard D. Irwin, Homewood, IL, 1979

Safire, William, *Language Maven Strikes Again,* Doubleday, New York, 1990. Can't get enough of his work.

Skillin, Marjorie E., *Words Into Type,* Prentice Hall, New York, 1974

Strunk, William Jr. and White, E. B., *Elements of Style,* Macmillan, New York, 1979. A classic.

Treece, Malra, *Communication For Business and the Professions,* Allyn and Bacon, Boston, MA, 1982. In touch with today's business writer.

_____ *Successful Business Writing,* Allyn and Bacon, Boston, MA, 1980

Williams, Joseph M., *Toward Clarity and Grace,* University of Chicago Press, Chicago, IL, 1990

Index